Classmates Extra:

Managing Your Classroom – Second Edition
by Gerard Dixie
Assessment: A Practical Guide for Secondary Teachers
by Howard Tanner and Sonia Jones

Lesson Planning

Second Edition

Graham Butt

continuum
LONDON • NEW YORK

Continuum International Publishing Group
The Tower Building
11 York Road
London SE1 7NX

80 Maiden Lane
Suite 704
New York
NY 10038

www.continuumbooks.com

British Library Cataloguing-in-Publication Data
A catalogue record for this book is available from the British Library.

ISBN 0-8264-8664-9 (paperback)

Typeset in 10/13pt Plantin by Originator Publishing Services, Gt Yarmouth
Printed and bound in Great Britain by Biddles Ltd, Guildford and King's Lynn

Contents

Contents

Preface

The aim of this book is to help you, as a teacher, to further your understanding of the principles of effective lesson planning. This will involve developing your knowledge of what promotes student learning, whilst also appreciating how different elements of the curriculum or examination specifications might be taught. The need to recognize the methods that can be used to teach particular subject content, the teaching resources that should be available to do so, and the ways in which these elements can be combined through careful planning, is therefore addressed.

Effective lesson preparation to ensure student learning is part of a cyclical process of planning, doing and evaluating. An important consideration will be how lesson evaluations link 'backwards' and 'forwards' throughout the planning process. It is essential that the reflective teacher understands where the students have 'come from' in terms of their learning, and where they should be 'going to' – space is therefore given to the appreciation of aspects of continuity and progression in planning. This will obviously involve an awareness of the role of assessment *of*, and *for*, learning and a reflection on a range of other factors pertinent to effective teaching, such as the ways in which successful classroom management can alter student behaviour and motivation.

The Importance of Effective Planning

Consider the words of Peter Hyman, previously a key strategist for the Blair government, who taught in a challenging Comprehensive School in London after leaving Downing Street in 2003. Having just started to plan lessons for the first time he offers these thoughts:

> These lessons give me a real insight into the extraordinary alchemy of teaching. One day it all works, I'm in good form, the students are focused, I think they are understanding the point, thinking for themselves. The next time, perhaps because I have done less preparation, perhaps because the students have had a bad day, the lesson is lacklustre, the students less sparky. For that hour though the class is in my hands. I am in charge, I can inspire or bore, shout or cajole, laugh or get fed up. It's all about pace, interest, variation. I can tell after a few lessons that I have stuck to the same formula for too long. I am becoming predictable. Instead of this being a different type of lesson that they look forward to, it's becoming a routine and I will have to change things round. ... What seems to be common to all teaching is the need for meticulous planning and pacy lessons that sweep the children along.
>
> (Hyman, 2005, p. 214)

To the lay observer good teaching looks remarkably straightforward. The impression, to the untrained eye at least, may be that the teacher merely has to turn up to the classroom and 'deliver' some subject content for the students in his or her charge to learn. The class is orderly, the teaching materials easily come to hand, the students respond appropriately to the questions or directives given by the teacher, and the learning atmosphere that results is supportive. The teacher is confident and assured, and the act of teaching appears almost effortless. Transitions between learning activities – all of which seem to be of interest to the students – are smooth and efficient. Questions posed by the teacher are considered seriously by the students who are eager to answer. They are, in turn, praised appropriately for the responses they make. There is little disruption or dispute, everyone seems to understand their role in this learning process and all go about the job in hand with a positive sense of purpose. What could be more straightforward?

However, these appearances are deceptive. The key to good teaching, purposeful class management and the achievement of sustained educational progress lies in effective planning. Learning does not occur by chance. It is therefore very rare (although perhaps not unknown) for a 'good lesson' to result from the teacher entering the classroom unprepared, without any procedure for the lesson being clearly planned beforehand. There is certainly substantial evidence to suggest that the opposite is more common – that poor teaching is usually linked to inadequate lesson planning. Experienced teachers who know their students well, who have built a rapport with them over time and who have a good understanding of the resources in their subject department may give the impression that they can successfully teach lessons that have barely been planned at all. Nonetheless, these teachers bring to the classroom pedagogic and subject-related knowledge that teachers rarely possess at the start of their careers. Most teachers who have taught successfully for a few years have built up a fund of lesson activities from which they can quickly select for different classes, instinctively knowing which activities will work best in which situations. There may be little evidence of formal 'paper planning' by experienced teachers, but this is often because their lesson planning is now an internalized procedure – a way of thinking and doing that has resulted from regular and extended contact with different groups of students within the context of teaching their subject. This was almost certainly *not* the case at the start of their teaching careers. Effective lesson planning takes time and a range of skills that all teachers need to master quickly, whether they are within their period of initial training or starting in a new school as a Newly Qualified Teacher (NQT).

Poor classroom practice, disruptive student behaviour, inadequate progression and poorly devised assessment tasks can all be linked back to some aspect of unsatisfactory planning. Underneath the surface of a good lesson lies a bedrock of teacher understanding about the principles of sound pedagogic practice. These principles are constructed from an appreciation of how children learn and from the self knowledge that results from being a reflective teacher, skilled in understanding why things happen in the classroom and how one might correct any problems that occur. Thus, successful lesson planning is linked to the evaluations of lessons previously taught – a circular relationship that helps to ensure good teaching and learning in both the short and long term. Interestingly, teachers who have problems in the classroom do not make this causal link back to their lesson planning. Many will blame the students – 'Nobody can teach that lot, they're well known for being disruptive,' 'I never bother doing groupwork with them because they never respond to it,' 'What's the point in planning anything for that class, they just don't want to learn!' – rather than recognizing that some teachers *do* manage to get such students learning. Again, this is not by chance – teachers who achieve learning, often with difficult groups, do so because of effective planning and preparation.

Worryingly, many new teachers claim that they have received little practical instruction about lesson planning, either during initial teacher training or during their induction as NQTs. Such claims are invariably incorrect – what is usually happening is that they either do not fully understand the advice given, or have difficulties interpreting this advice within a particular educational setting. This may result in beginning teachers, and their mentors, becoming frustrated. It may appear that advice is not being heeded, or that giving guidance on planning to beginning teachers is fruitless because what works in the classroom for one teacher does not for another. Teaching is, after all, a highly personal activity. However, there are broad similarities between the practices of good teachers in the classroom, just as there are similarities between the approaches they adopt to achieve effective lesson planning and preparation.

The planning process

Many teachers, particularly those at the start of their teaching careers, find lesson planning problematic and overly time consuming. They not only discover that the practicalities of planning are difficult, but also attempt to plan having not yet sufficiently developed a language and set of concepts relevant to the planning process. Experienced teachers tend to forget just how difficult planning is for a beginning teacher – especially as the main experience the new teacher has of lessons is still one of *being* taught, rather than of actually *teaching*. New teachers tend to have been taught effectively and are 'successes' of the education system (in as much that they have progressed through their education to a stage when they themselves are training to teach). As a consequence the new teacher may see nothing wrong in attempting to adopt similar styles of teaching to the ones they experienced as learners. However, using this approach to planning is fraught with dangers; not least in that 'good teaching' is difficult to break down into constituent sections by inexperienced teachers. Also merely attempting to copy, or mimic, a teaching style will often simply not work.

One of the main difficulties when planning lessons is achieving a clear definition of what we, as teachers, are trying to convey to students about our subject. Are we trying to teach the students specific content, facts, concepts or skills? How will these be received by a given group of students, of a particular age and range of abilities? Are the students ready for our chosen approach(es) to teaching? Viewing your subject from the perspective of the *learner* is a difficult process – as teachers we should know and understand the content of the subject we teach, but thinking carefully about how this could be conveyed to students in a supportive, interesting and dynamic way is the essence of good lesson planning.

In many ways curriculum documents, national curricula and syllabuses only give limited support to the teacher when planning lessons. They often consist of lists of content and concepts, but give little indication of the planning steps necessary to achieve successful delivery in the classroom. This implies that the teacher has to have a full appreciation both of their subject and of a range of teaching methods before attempting to teach. Again, seeing things from the perspective of the learner is key. What might learners find difficult to understand or do? Why might lessons be proving hard for them? How might I plan to approach particular aspects of the subject to make them more digestable? It is advisable to look closely at the subject content of each lesson, or of a series of lessons, as a prerequisite of the planning process. This comes before the planning of particular teaching and learning styles which one feels will be most appropriate for a lesson.

The types of difficulties that teachers have with planning lessons varies considerably. It is not simply the case that bright, talented and well-motivated teachers find their lessons easy to plan – or that teachers who adopt a more 'laissez faire' approach are poor planners, and therefore ineffectual teachers. Many exceptionally gifted and charismatic teachers face real problems when trying to plan out what will happen in their classrooms – they may be able to capture students' attention and be good at helping them learn, but have comparatively little idea about how to plan for this learning over a series of lessons, or even within a single lesson. Also, some teachers who find planning, preparation and delivery straightforward with most classes, may have particular problems when faced with planning for certain themes, or for certain abilities of students.

2

Key Factors in Lesson Planning

A number of factors need to be considered in the planning process. Some of these may be fairly obvious and straightforward, but are nonetheless factors that will need to be considered for each lesson. Others may apply only within the first few lessons that you teach a new group, or when you encounter an unfamiliar learning situation. When you are planning to teach difficult groups or new topics, or when introducing a previously untried teaching method, planning may be more complex and require a much deeper understanding of education theory. You will certainly need to have some knowledge of the following:

- the capabilities of the students you are going to teach;
- what you think the students should be learning;
- the ways in which you feel they will learn best.

If possible, it helps to observe each group of students before you teach them. This may enable you to plan the first few lessons more successfully – however, gaining the time to undertake such observation is a luxury that is generally unavailable to teachers. Failing this, discussing the nature of the group with their previous teacher will help, although you will need to be sensitive to the fact that all teachers not only teach differently but also appraise the strengths and weaknesses of groups and individual students differently. Such 'surface' knowledge is helpful when starting your lesson planning, but nothing can replace the knowledge gained from actually teaching a group. Therefore information gathering before the event can only take you so far. It is also important to realize that the foundations that underpin good planning link to deeper knowledge and understanding of how groups and individuals learn, of appropriate subject knowledge for the age and abilities of the students, and an appreciation of the importance of assessment *for* learning.

Let us therefore consider a preliminary list of the questions that you might need to take into account when starting to plan lessons:

- What is the scheme of work that the students are following?
- What has been taught and learnt in the previous lesson(s)?
- What do you want the students to learn in the lesson you are planning (and in future lessons)?
- How will your lesson plan facilitate learning?
- What resources will you need?
- What activities will the students undertake?

Three further questions will need to be posed after the planned lesson has been taught:

- How will you know what the students have learnt (assessment)?
- How will you know how effective the lesson has been from your perspective as the teacher and the students' perspective as learners (evaluation)?
- What action will you need to take in future lessons to ensure that effective learning is taking place?

In essence, these questions break down into considerations of four major components of the lesson and how it should be planned:

1. The *purpose* of the lesson (the aims, objectives and expected learning outcomes).
2. The *substance* of the lesson (the subject knowledge, understanding and skills).
3. The *methods* of the lesson (the strategies employed to ensure learning).
4. The *evaluation* of the lesson (of student learning and teacher teaching).

These components are underpinned by an even broader range of considerations that may also be phrased as questions: How do students learn? What are the best ways to match one's teaching to the different 'abilities' of students? What are the most appropriate forms of assessment in the classroom? Although these questions may not be directly 'answerable' for each specific learning event in every lesson you will need to appreciate why such generic questions are important.

Schemes of work

The first question that you might need to consider when starting to plan lessons is: What is the scheme of work that the students are following? Before delving into the intricacies of single lesson planning it is important to recognize that lesson plans should 'nest' within a larger scheme of work which has been previously devised by your subject department. These schemes, which are sometimes broken down into 'units of work', are essential to the planning process. National Curriculum subjects each have 'programmes of study', whilst examination awarding bodies provide subject 'specifications' (or previously 'syllabuses') from which schools can create their own schemes of work. Each scheme is essentially an overall plan, usually for a term or half a term of the academic year, for teachers to follow outlining the content, methods and resources that will be used to deliver the subject curriculum. From each scheme of work a number of lesson plans for individual lessons will be devised which, when taken together, add up to the delivery of a specific section of the curriculum or specifications. In effect a scheme of work therefore provides a route through some aspect of the curriculum indicating to the teacher particular opportunities for students to learn. This relationship is illustrated in Figure 2.1.

It is important that schemes of work, as well as the lessons planned from them, take account of the learning that has occurred previously and that which will (hopefully) occur in the future. In this way teachers must be mindful of both continuity and progression within their subject.

Essentially, the term 'continuity' refers to the maintenance and development of certain aspects of a subject, and the ways

Level	Activity	Initial outcomes
School	1. Formulate general policies for the whole curriculum.	General policy statements. Guidance on specific aspects. School timetable.
Subject department or course team	2. Formulate policies for subject. 3. Devise schemes of work for courses. 4. Plan and prepare units of study.	Policy statements and guidelines for subject. Schemes of work and rationale for each course. Plans for units of work.
Individual teachers	5. Plan and prepare lessons.	Lesson plans and teaching materials.

Figure 2.1 Overview of the relationship between the curriculum, schemes of work and lesson plans
(after Bennetts, 1996)

in which they are taught, through a sequence of lessons. Thus, continuity may make reference to the following:

- the aims of the subject, which are maintained across the Key Stages and beyond;
- the sections of subject content, including particular themes or concepts that are central to the subject;
- types of teaching and learning activities;
- methodology, involving students undertaking particular tasks or adopting particular approaches to their learning over a period of time;
- working relationships amongst the students, for example if they might be expected to work with a particular partner or group;
- assessment procedures;
- recording/profiling of achievement.

The aim of establishing continuity is to allow students to build upon their previous educational experiences in a subject – experiences that continue as they pass through their period of formal education.

'Progression' refers to the measurable advances that students make in their knowledge, understanding and skills in a subject over time. As such, there should be an ordered hierarchy of each of these aspects of learning within the curriculum and within the schemes of work that have been devised. The pace at which students progress obviously varies according to their individual aptitude, ability and intelligence – concepts that are not straightforward and whose meanings are contested within the world of education (for example, is one's intelligence level 'fixed' and therefore incapable of being improved upon through the process of education?). Whilst there is not space here to debate these issues in depth it is important to realize that your personal philosophy of education and views on student learning will affect how you choose to plan to teach. Progression can be described as an increase in the:

- complexity of the concepts to be understood;
- level of skills to be obtained;
- level of thinking to be applied;
- difficulty of the problems to be solved;
- autonomy of the learner (for example, a reduction in teacher support and scaffolding of learning over time).

In short, it implies a movement for the student from 'low order' thinking (mainly knowledge recall and comprehension) to 'high order' thinking (mainly application, synthesis and evaluation). During this journey students should be encouraged to engage in metacognition, that is 'thinking about thinking', to ensure that they understand and can contribute to their educational progress. Progression is usually monitored through different forms of assessment. However, it is a complex and non linear process – students can go 'backwards' in their learning as well as 'forwards', requiring periods of revision and consolidation. The Level Descriptions within each of the National Curriculum subjects have been designed to try to encapsulate elements of both continuity and progression within the subjects. The levels do this by describing typical student performance with respect to knowledge, understanding and skills within each subject.

It is a truism that schemes of work, and the curricula or specifications from which they are developed, need to be regularly updated to ensure their continuing relevance and applicability. In today's rapidly changing world it would be foolish to assume that the schemes of work planned for many subjects as little as two or three years ago will still be wholly appropriate for students about to enter university, further education or their first job. In some subjects (such as geography, citizenship and 'general studies') schemes of work may need to be significantly updated annually to take account of contemporary events.

Schemes of work can be produced in a variety of slightly different formats, as can lesson plans. However, the majority of schemes aim to provide similar sorts of information for the teacher and attempt to serve as an overall guide to lesson planning.

Most schemes of work will therefore contain some statements on:

1. *Aims and objectives* – what the scheme is trying to achieve in terms of subject knowledge, understanding, skills, and values and attitudes to be learnt. These aims may be taken directly from the National Curriculum Subject Orders, or from examination specifications, or be partly of the subject department's own devising. There may be some 'fine tuning' within the schemes into more achievable learning objectives, but this level of detail is often left to individual lesson plans.

2. *Content* – the primary function of a scheme of work is to present sections of subject content to be taught and learnt. Each section should be coherent and have a clear focus. This may involve providing a very brief overview of the actual lessons that will be taught. Some indication is often given about teaching and learning methods or educational events that may have particular relevance to the delivery of some aspect of subject content, e.g. a field trip or visit, work outside the classroom, a particular project, etc. An indication is sometimes provided of the subject content that has gone before and that which will follow (see continuity and progression) such that a sequence of learning is established. Remember that the National Curriculum Programmes of Study only afford a guide to the minimum knowledge, understanding and skills that students should attain during each Key Stage – they are not a detailed indicator of the

specific content of the lesson plans to be created, more a framework for you to work within. Similar statements apply to specifications from examination awarding bodies.

3. *Timings* – how many lessons are available to teach the scheme. These estimates are usually conservative, for the length of the school terms and half terms currently vary (consider how long the Autumn Term is in most schools compared to the Spring Term!). Teaching time will invariably be 'lost' to whole school events such as examinations, fire drills, other subjects' trips or special events. It is also worth remembering that the overall time allocation given to different subjects can vary quite considerably from school to school.

4. *Resources* – key resources available to teach the scheme (or an indication of those which will need to be produced). Resources not only refer to those materials used in the process of teaching and learning, but also to the staff available to carry out the teaching – these include both departmental staff and classroom assistants/teaching assistants. Different subjects often have radically different key resources for teaching and learning. For example, a PE department will be using very different teaching resources to a Maths department.

5. *Assessment* – this is often somewhat neglected at the planning stage, but it is essential for effective teaching and learning (both assessment *of* learning and assessment *for* learning). It is very important that schemes of work detail key assessment opportunities and convey the purposes of these assessments. Remember that there are both teacher assessments (usually 'low stakes') as well as external assessments (usually 'high stakes'). There is a fundamental difference between formative and summative assessment. The need for assessment planning is made all the more crucial given the importance placed on progression, evidence of which is often gained through assessment.

6. *Cross curricular links* – many curriculum subjects will 'interface' to some extent with other areas of learning. For example, both the Geography and Science National Curriculum can cover aspects of physical weathering and rock formation at Key Stage 3, whilst the ICT curriculum has considerable overlap with the requirements to teach ICT through other subjects (for example, how to use a computer, working with databases, spreadsheets, the Internet, etc.). Citizenship may be delivered through a variety of subject areas all of which will need to have some understanding of what the others are doing. Such links should be clearly stated on the schemes of work devised.

There may also be information within the scheme of work on safety procedures and preferred teaching methods. However, by their very nature, schemes of work should be concise documents designed to give an overview of the learning experience for one part of the subject-based curriculum (see Figure 2.2). The fine detail of the process of teaching and learning should be saved for the individual lesson plans.

When planning lessons based on schemes of work similar headings may be used to those given above, but now with reference to single teaching and learning episodes (that is, the individual lessons), rather than a whole collection of lessons. A scheme of work provides a customized guide to a particular element of a Programme of Study or specification and how it might be taught by yourself and members of your subject department. The scheme should therefore be more personal, 'fine tuned' and practical than the original documents from which it has been created, but should not carry the amount of detail necessary to teach an individual lesson. A problem for many beginning teachers is that they have not been involved in the original planning of the scheme of work which, as a result, may seem to be rather detached from the lessons they have to plan.

Course: Geography KS3   Year: 7
Unit of study: Volcanic activity

Time: 6 weeks

Learning objectives:

1. Know about the scale of volcanic activity.
2. Recognize and describe volcanic landforms – lava flows, volcanic cones and craters.
3. Explain how particular types of landforms are related to types of eruption.
4. Understand the nature and impact of hazards associated with volcanic eruptions.
5. Explain how the global distribution of active volcanoes is related to the pattern of crustal plates.
6. Make effective use of a range of source materials.

Contribution to cross curricular themes:

Information Technology: using IT to obtain, select, organize and present information.

Links with other subjects:

English: writing for different purposes – description (volcanic landforms); reporting (an eruption, hazards); explanation (causes of volcanic activity).

Science: some links with the earth science component.

Time	Content	Learning activities and teaching methods	Resource materials
2 weeks	1. Case study of three volcanic eruptions illustrating contrasts (e.g. ....).	Watch video; examine photographs and maps; read accounts of the eruptions. Compare the eruptions; identify the types of materials emitted; describe landforms.	Video (. . . . .) Textbook (. . . . .) Rock specimens

1 week	2. Volcanic landforms – lava flows, volcanic cones and craters.	Identify and make notes on the factors which influence the shape of volcanoes; draw and annotate diagrams.	Display of photographs and newspaper reports
2 weeks	3. Volcanic eruptions as natural hazards; the possibilities and difficulties of predicting eruptions. Why do people live in volcanic areas?	Use IT to produce a newspaper report of an eruption – small groups.	IT software (. . . . .)
1 week	4. Global distribution of active volcanoes.	Examine world maps to compare distribution of earthquakes, volcanoes, fold mountains, and crustal plates. Teacher leads pupils towards simple explanations; pupils record the explanations with guidance.	Maps
			Textbooks
	5. Explanation of distribution pattern.		Differentiated worksheets

Methods of assessment	Evaluation of unit
Routine monitoring of pupils' work, with particular attention given to the newspaper report, and to pupils' explanations of volcanic landforms and the global distribution pattern.	Evaluation to be written soon after the completion of the unit, and following discussions between the teachers.

Figure 2.2 Example of a scheme of work
(after Bennetts, 1996)

Lesson planning

As a beginning teacher you will usually be given fairly clear guidelines as to the subject content you are expected to teach. This content, and to an extent the teaching methods and assessment of learning that might go with it, will have been outlined for you in a variety of ways. In general the curriculum taught within schools is determined externally – for example at Key Stage 3 all students must follow a programme of study related to the National Curriculum. Those students who later follow a GCSE syllabus designed by an examination awarding body, and then a specification for AS/A2 level after the age of 16, also pursue an externally determined educational pathway. However, the interpretation of these curriculum documents and specifications, as reflected in the departmental schemes of work, is a matter of professional judgement exercised by individual teachers within the subject department. Some schools interpret the content of the curriculum 'closely' and have detailed schemes of work that all teachers must follow; others interpret it 'loosely' and leave the translation of the curriculum largely to the individual teacher, having previously established its broad parameters. The purpose of the lesson plan is to provide a practical and usable guide to the teaching and learning activities that will occur within a particular lesson.

Figure 2.3 indicates the process of starting to plan for a particular Maths topic which will cover a number of lessons. The 'topic overview' provides the framework for a series of interconnected lesson plans. Each of the lessons taught is evaluated and the information gained is used to support the planning of subsequent lessons, and of the unit as a whole. One good piece of advice is to think about planning for a sequence of lessons, rather than seeing lessons as a number of 'one-offs'. In this way you, and more importantly the students, will see the continuity and progression of the lessons you have planned.

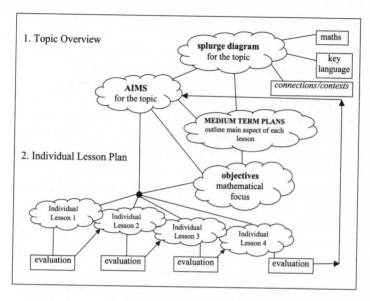

Figure 2.3 Initial planning for a series of Maths lessons on a given topic
(Prestage, Perks and Hewitt, 2005)

The subject content of each of the lessons is closely linked to the topic. One approach to clarifying and then defining the lesson content is to create a 'splurge diagram' (see Figure 2.4) to investigate the interconnections within and around that topic. This is an important first step in the planning process, leading (with support) to some decisions about what the aims, objectives and content will be for a series of lessons.

The methods by which teachers actually teach their lessons are not usually closely defined either by the curriculum, specification or departmental diktat. It is therefore the professional responsibility of each teacher to apply the methods which personally suit their teaching style and also to take account of the ways in which their students learn. We know that students have

Lesson Planning

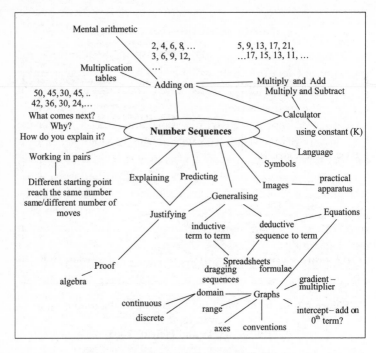

Figure 2.4 Example of a 'splurge' diagram
(Prestage, Perks and Hewitt, 2005)

different preferred learning styles – this implies that teachers should adopt a variety of teaching methods. An essential part of the process of learning how to teach involves experimenting, as well as evaluating a range of teaching strategies and approaches from the perspective of the learner. In conclusion it is useful to reflect on the fact that in state schools *what* is taught is usually closely defined by the National Curriculum or specifications from the awarding bodies, whilst *how* this content is taught is largely determined through the professional judgement of the individual teacher.

Some planning formats

A lesson plan is a concise, working document which outlines the teaching and learning that will be conducted within a single lesson. It is a practical instrument which should be used within the lesson as an *aide memoire* and can follow a standard format, often reproduced within departments as a *pro forma*. The lesson plan should 'fit' within the broader scheme of work and be written in such a way that it is clear to another teacher (or observer) what is intended within the lesson – the plan should be 'teachable' by another teacher; it should also be possible for another teacher to watch your lesson and then construct a similar plan simply by observing what happened at different times in the lesson! A lesson plan is not a script to be read out (although it may contain appended notes on the subject content to be covered in the lesson) and should not be followed slavishly if events within the classroom mean that a change in direction for you and your students is advisable and justifiable on educational grounds. Moving from one learning activity to the next before the first activity is finished properly, and just because the lesson you have planned states that after ten minutes a change of activity is due, is not good teaching. (Although grossly misjudging the amount of time an activity takes is similarly not good planning!)

A variety of suggestions for lesson plan formats are given in Figure 2.6 (see pages 109 to 128 for examples of completed lesson plans for a range of National Curriculum subjects). The exact form of the lesson plan you adopt is very much a personal choice: however, note that all lesson plans contain similar common elements, such as aims, learning objectives, teaching and learning activities, timings, assessment and evaluation. Many include simple 'administrative' details such as the date, classroom, information about the class/year group, number of students of each sex, class register, and possibly an appended seating plan. It is most important that you are clear about what the students should know, understand and be able to do as a result of your planned lesson being taught. Considering which activities students will engage in to achieve this learning is obviously a key to the planning process. In many lessons it will be possible to share the learning objectives, expected outcomes and criteria for success with the students. In this way students will be able to take some responsibility for their learning and will not be entirely reliant on you for guidance and success. Each of the lesson plans has a range of 'features' that can be briefly explained as follows:

- *Aims* – the overall purpose of the lesson(s), a broad statement of educational intentions (in the particular subject taught). The aims are usually more general than the learning objectives and encapsulate the overall 'direction' of the learning that will take place. Aims provide the context for the lessons, which are in turn more closely defined and described by the learning objectives.
- *Learning objectives* – specific goals or purposes to be achieved, targets for students' learning in this lesson. Objectives help to narrow down the aims of the scheme of work or syllabus/ specifications into a more workable form. In many schools the teacher is encouraged to state the lesson aims and/or learning objectives for the students at the start of the lesson, often displaying these for the class on a whiteboard or OHP transparency. This is a good idea as it clarifies the purpose of the lesson and explains to students what they should achieve by the end of the lesson.

Establishing the learning objectives for the educational journey your students are about to make is a fundamental aspect of planning. Having already discovered roughly where the students 'are at' in their knowledge, understanding and skills you need to determine where they will 'go to' next and how they will get there. The analogy of the students catching a train or a bus is a useful one – if the teacher (or train/bus driver) does not stop at the right places and then deliver the students to the correct destinations in their learning they will not be able to complete their educational journey. (Travelling too fast or too slow may also create problems!) The 'stops', 'destinations' and 'modes of travel' in the learning process can all be articulated through the learning objectives.

When devising learning objectives it is important to remember that although these will largely determine what you teach, and often the ways in which you teach, they primarily concentrate on the students' *learning*. They are not *teaching* objectives. This may seem like a moot point – however, in your planning it is important to concentrate on what the students will learn, and by what point (end of this lesson? end of a series of lessons?) they will have learnt it. It is also important to consider how you will recognize, assess and measure this learning, rather than being too exercised by what *you* will teach them. Importantly, the most effective teachers see lesson planning as more of a 'student centred', rather than 'teacher centred', activity – that is, they are more concerned when planning with thinking about facilitating the activities the *students* will be doing in their lessons, than about how they will be performing in front of their audience of students.

Because of this important distinction it will be wise when planning lessons to remind yourself of the primacy of the learner. This can be achieved by writing out learning objectives in the following way on your lesson plan:

By the end of the lesson students will:

- **know that** ... (knowledge: factual information, for example names, places, symbols, formulae, events)

- **develop/be able to** ... (skills: using knowledge, applying techniques, analysing information, etc.)
- **understand how/why** ... (understanding: concepts, reasons, effects, principles, processes, etc.)
- **develop/be aware of** ... (attitudes and values: empathy, caring, sensitivity towards social issues, feelings, moral issues, etc.)

(DfES/QCA, 2002, p. 72)

It is desirable to share the learning objectives with the students (obviously using language they will readily understand) and to identify the learning outcomes that will demonstrate that they have successfully achieved their learning. Teachers are regularly advised to write the aim, or learning objective, of each lesson on the board to share with the students at the start of each lesson. This is an admirable practice, as long as the teacher provides enough time to fully explain the objectives rather than them merely wanting them to be copied down, alongside the day's date and the lesson title. Learning objectives do not necessarily have to be written down and displayed by the teacher. They could be introduced through structured question and answer, a suitably devised starter activity, whole class discussion, or prioritizing a card sort. Students will be more confident and engaged with their learning if they have some notion of *why* they are learning, what they are learning, and where they will end up as a result.

The learning objectives can be modelled within a diagram (see Figure 2.5) which indicates how they fit into the whole process of planning a lesson.

Learning objectives should be phrased as concise, clear and achievable statements. We have already noted the use of phrases such as: 'Students should be able to ...', 'Students will know how to ...', 'Students will understand that ...'.

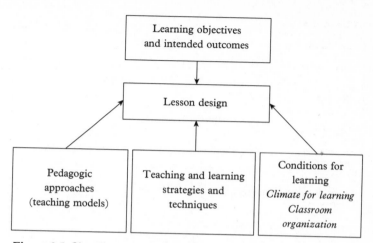

Figure 2.5 Showing how learning objectives/outcomes fit within the process of lesson planning
(DfES, 2004)

However, you may also wish to use words that clarify the nature of the students' task, such as 'describe', 'classify', 'compare and contrast', 'list', 'understand', 'decide', 'differentiate between'. These learning objectives may relate to knowledge, understanding, skills and/or values and attitudes (that is, the cognitive, behavioural and affective elements of learning). When devising learning objectives always think about what you are expecting the *students* to be able to do and write the statements in such a way that they will understand what is expected of them. It is also important to consider how the outcomes of these objectives might be measured. Evaluation of the success, or otherwise, of your lesson will clearly link back to whether your learning objectives have been achieved.

With difficult classes your learning objectives may relate more to classroom management, and the maintenance of

Lesson Planning

(a) Lesson Plan 'A'

Day/Period   Year group

Aim of lesson

Objectives

Unit of work

Resources

Methods/procedures (timings)

Homework

Evaluation

Figure 2.6 Examples of lesson plan formats

(b) Lesson Plan 'B'

Day/Period	Year group
Aim of lesson	
Objectives	
Unit of work	
Resources	
Methods/procedures (timings)	
Teacher activities	Student activities
Homework	
Evaluation	

Lesson Planning

(c) Lesson Plan 'C'

Day/Period	Year group
Aim of lesson	
Objectives	(1) Subject ideas/concepts (2) Subject skills (3) Values & attitudes
Subject content	
Unit of work	
Equipment and resources	
Methods/procedures (timings)	
Teacher activities	Student activities
Homework	
Evaluation	

Figure 2.6 (*cont.*)

(d) Lesson Plan 'D'

Date	Lesson	Time	Class	Room

Title of lesson

Lesson's aims

Learning objectives and enquiry questions

Subject content: National Curriculum/syllabus links	Cross curricular links/themes/ competences
Resources	Advance preparation (room and equipment)
Differentiation	Action points

Learning activities/tasks	Time	Teaching strategies/actions

Assessment opportunities, objectives and evidence

Evaluation of learning	Evaluation of teaching

Action points

Lesson Planning

(e) Lesson Plan 'E'

Date	Time	Room	Number in group	Class	Age group/s

Subject/topic/focus of activity

Context of the learning activity

Learning objectives for students	My own professional learning objectives

Learning processes of the activity	Resources	Timing	Teacher actions, including content and management

Evaluation and possible targets

Figure 2.6 (*cont.*)

(f) Lesson Plan 'F'

Class Date Time Room Subject/topic	Lesson objectives	
	Knowledge and understanding	Skills, attitudes and values
Action points brought forward		Links with National Curriculum PoS if appropriate
Resources, equipment and room preparation		
Learning task/activity, including resource/s to be used	Time	Teacher action/s, including content focus
Evaluation of learning, including objectives	Evaluation of teaching, including planning, preparation, management and communication	
Action points to carry forward		

acceptable standards of behaviour in the classroom, than to subject content or concepts.

- *Subject content* – determined by the National Curriculum Subject Orders, GCSE or AS/A2 level followed, but mediated through departmental schemes and units of work. Importantly the *mode* of delivery of this content is a professional choice for the individual teacher.

Expertise within their subject is essential for any teacher, but it does not automatically follow that any teacher who possesses such knowledge will be effective in helping the students to learn. Many teachers have extensive, 'deep' subject knowledge in some areas, but 'broad' or even superficial knowledge in others – often requiring them to learn aspects of subject content that they have never encountered before. This obviously has an effect on lesson planning. Transforming your subject knowledge, however recently gained, into learning activities appropriate for younger students is not straightforward. Nonetheless this process lies at the heart of effective planning.

Teachers who are not confident about aspects of their subject knowledge sometimes attach 'crib notes' to their lesson plans to support them if difficulties occur. This is acceptable, but gives rise to the temptation to read directly from a sheet – an act which rarely conveys confidence to a group of students. Similarly, teachers who try to script what they are going to say in a lesson invariably appear wooden, inflexible and unresponsive.

- *Learning activities* – a sequence of 'phases for learning' in the lesson, from beginning to end. Statements of learning activities imply making a choice of the most productive ways in which you think the students will learn – such activities should be designed to deliver the previously stated learning objectives.

This suggests that a variety of possible overall structures

for any particular lesson may exist. For example, the most basic structure would be a simple 'three part' lesson, which began with some form of starter activity, had a main activity in the next phase and ended with a plenary:

starter	main activity	plenary

To increase variety and challenge, the lesson might be structured with more than one main activity and a single, final plenary:

starter	first main activity	short plenary	second main activity	longer plenary

Many lessons would be more complex still. These would involve a variety of 'starts', 'transitions', 'activities' and 'plenaries' where there may also be some differentiated tasks and opportunities for whole class, group, paired or individual work.

starter	first activity – whole class	first plenary	second acivity – paired work	pairs' feedback	third activity – groups	second plenary	fourth activity

(after DfES, 2002)

The advantage of the more complex lesson plans is that they provide opportunities for a greater variety of teaching and learning methods to be used. This usually implies that the different needs of the learners will be catered for and that the range of preferred learning styles that exist within the class will, to some extent, be met.

You can see from the models above that all lessons have – at the very least – a 'start', a 'middle' and an 'end'. This seems an obvious point. However, many teachers make the mistake, often as a result of poor or insufficient planning, of delivering lessons where one of these elements is missing. They either launch into the main activity too quickly, without having set it up correctly, with the students left bewildered as to what is happening and what they should be doing: an example of a lesson with an inadequate 'start'. Or, they let the starter activities drift on too long, leaving an inadequate amount of time to set up and progress through the main activity: a lesson with a poor 'middle' (and possibly poor 'end'). Or, they spend too long on the starter and/or main activity and as a result conclude the lesson in a hurried fashion: a lesson with no proper 'end'. Effective planning, with a sensible set of timings for each of these phases of the lesson, will help to eradicate these all too common problems.

Students respond best when they know where they are going in a lesson and how they are going to get there. With many lessons now stretching over 70 minutes – a long time for anybody to give their undivided attention and focus – it may be best to break the lesson down into bite-sized chunks. The key to success is therefore not to let any activity go on too long and to have a variety of different tasks for students to complete. Some teachers mentally divide their lessons up when planning into discrete halves or thirds precisely to combat this issue.

Learning activities can be either 'student centred' or 'teacher centred', but should be designed to engage and motivate the students, and to have challenge and pace. A variety of supporting strategies can be employed related to these activities: to introduce the lesson, 'hook' students, encourage a sound working atmosphere, conclude activities, and problem solve. The activities must be differentiated according to the needs of the students in the group (see O'Brien and Guiney, 2001). It should be remembered that for any learning activity the teacher will need to introduce the task, ensure that all students understand the task and can cope with it, clarify and explain the resources to be used, and introduce any new vocabulary. At the end of the activity/lesson there should be a review of what has been learnt, an opportunity for target setting, and a clarification of links forward to the next lesson(s) and future learning.

Many learning activities involve the teacher posing questions for the students to respond to, either orally or in written form. The art of good questioning is beyond the scope of this book; however, it is important to consider the types of questions that you must ask to promote student learning. This has relevance in the planning stage, for just as some teachers append 'crib notes' of subject content to their lesson plans, some may also wish to have a note of 'key questions' they wish to pose. Teachers sometimes find that oral 'question and answer' sessions do not go as well as they had hoped, perhaps being taken in directions by their students' answers they had not anticipated or because they have not asked the 'right' questions. Planning key questions beforehand will help to keep the learning on track.

- *Health and safety* – for a number of subjects considerations of health and safety are a key component of lesson planning. Certain lessons will carry some element of risk which should obviously be minimized. The subjects most commonly associated with potential risks are the Sciences and PE: however, there may be risks at certain times within other subject areas. For example, in English during lessons that incorporate activities such as drama, in Geography and History during field trips – indeed in any subject that is conducting an 'off site' experience. In subjects where a risk element often occurs guidelines are available from the DfES, from the LEA in which the school is located, from the school and often from the subject department itself.
- *Resources* – these may either be departmental (i.e. resources

previously prepared by a member of the department and kept for the use of all staff), or 'hardware' (worksheets, textbooks, audio visual equipment, computers, etc., will fall within this category) – or personal. Personal resources are those that you will devise for teaching a particular group, with due consideration of its particular needs. Always make sure that if you intend to use departmental resources they will be available when you want them and within the classroom you are expected to teach in! Equipment may need to be 'booked' some time in advance of the lesson, so make yourself aware of the necessary arrangements to do so within your department and follow them closely.

- *Timings* – all lesson plans should clearly detail when different activities are due to occur in the lesson. Achieving an accurate prediction of how long different activities will take, and as a result being confident about when transitions will occur in the lesson and when the lesson should end, is very important. Although it is not necessary to keep slavishly to the timings you have worked out you should be aware that allowing activities to 'drift on' for too long will have a major impact on students' attentiveness and their capacity for learning. When 'drifting' occurs towards the end of a lesson this may mean a very rushed conclusion to the lesson and as a result a loss of control. You should consider that teaching is not a wholly predictable activity and that learning opportunities may arise unexpectedly within a lesson. Clearly you can not be expected to have thought about all eventualities beforehand. You may choose to seize the opportunity, divert from your planned lesson and take time to do something different. This is quite acceptable, as long as what results is beneficial to student learning. A wholly spontaneous, high-risk, unprepared deviation from your carefully thought-through lesson plan into an educational cul-de-sac from which manoeuvre is problematic is not advisable!

It is worthwhile briefly considering the amount of time that you will be given to teach your subject to different groups by your school, as this has a direct impact on what can be planned, taught and learnt. The overall curriculum time given to each subject, and the distribution of periods into which this time is divided (the lessons), is largely decided upon by individual schools. Therefore a history teacher, say, in one school may find that she has 70 minutes each week to teach her subject to each of her classes in Key Stage 3, whilst a teacher in a neighbouring school may be given 90 minutes per week to teach the same curriculum. This obviously has an effect on what can be covered in the time available, particularly if this time is distributed into two lessons throughout each week rather than being concentrated into a 'double' lesson.

There has been a recent trend in some schools of reducing the overall number of lessons to be taught, concentrating learning into fewer, longer sessions. Some teachers believe that this is not entirely beneficial for all students. Admittedly the 'practical' subjects, such as PE, Sciences and Technology, can greatly benefit from longer lesson times – as indeed do many other subjects that wish to employ activities such as games, role plays, decision-making exercises and simulations. However, in many curriculum areas these long periods of time can actually be anti educational. There is some evidence that shorter lessons can lead to more focused, purposeful teaching and learning, whilst longer lessons may be typified by less focused, more one-paced and less dynamic learning episodes. During longer lessons certain students simply find that the act of learning becomes boring.

- *Assessment* – consideration of the assessment of students' learning is integral to the planning of effective lessons. Assessment may be both formal (through set work, exercises, outcomes of activities, oral question and answer, testing) and informal (general monitoring of students' progress, working atmosphere in the lesson, discussion with students). Assessment should help you to determine whether your planned learning objectives have been met.

- *Evaluation* – a critical reflection on both your teaching and your students' learning (for a much fuller exploration of lesson evaluation see Section 6).

What choices do we have?

It may appear, at first sight, that teachers have little choice about what, and indeed how, they teach. If this is true then the planning process – and the teaching that results – should be relatively straightforward. However, even when teaching the most restrictive and closely defined syllabus the ways in which we choose to teach are entirely our own. There is never a single 'right' way of teaching. Each area of content, each skill, topic and theme opens up a variety of possibilities of how it could be taught. The art of planning is to choose which approach is best suited to the circumstances in which you will teach. This highlights a major difference between the beginning teacher and the experienced teacher – the latter can often see a variety of potential approaches to teaching the same content and is prepared to both plan and adapt these according to circumstances. Experienced teachers also tend not to be wedded to a lesson plan that fails to 'deliver', but can quickly and skilfully adapt their approach to gain the maximum learning potential from a lesson. As such, for them, the planning process is fluid and ongoing – responding to the signals and situations of the classroom in a dynamic, almost organic, way.

3

Planning for Difference

In the introductory chapter of their book on differentiation Tim O'Brien and Dennis Guiney remind us that:

> We cannot assume that just because a teacher teaches a learner learns what was intended. The process is far more complex than one of received input and intended outcome. This is because teachers, when engaging with learners, are not involved in programming machines; the learning process involves humans who are diverse in their needs, development, attitudes, values and beliefs.
>
> (O'Brien and Guiney, 2001, p. 2)

Didactic models of teaching and learning, where the teacher simply transmits the knowledge for the learner to learn, often carry assumptions that all learners are basically similar. Such models imply that students possess common capabilities, capacities and motivations to learn. They also conveniently assume that all students learn at the same pace. This is obviously untrue, as observation of almost any lesson will show!

Learners need to be able to handle the lesson content that is presented to them. They have to be able to understand it, process it, apply it and store it. They will have to transact this knowledge with the teacher and with their peers. They may also have to reform it and 'pass it on' in some way. This usually implies an active, rather than a passive, process. Simply listening to the teacher will only rarely constitute effective learning for most students. The teacher has to plan and prepare for all the students in the class – an act of differentiation. If the teacher fails to plan for differentiation someone in the class will miss out – although the teacher must always be aware that one cannot focus differentiation on one group without having some impact on the rest of the class. In our planning we must think not only of the differentiation of resources, but also of the differentiation of teaching strategies, methods, language, focus, class management and assessment.

O'Brien and Guiney propose a number of 'principles for differentiation' and point out that successful differentiation is not about planning to troubleshoot for some students, but must be a practice that is applied to all. The principles they state are:

- all children have a right to high quality education;
- every child can learn;
- every teacher can learn;
- learning is a process that involves mutual relationships;
- progress for all will be expected, recognized and rewarded;
- people and learning systems can change for the better.

It is therefore essential at an early stage of lesson planning to consider the aptitudes and abilities of the students you will be teaching. Differentiation is primarily the targeting of teaching and learning materials, and pedagogy, for different abilities of students. It will certainly help to make your lessons more applicable to the students you teach and will enable you to devise learning activities and resources for students who have particular abilities, attention spans, behavioural issues and learning needs. However, differentiation is not a straightforward task given the almost infinite variety of preferred learning styles and educational demands within any group of students. Your aim should be to keep *all* students engaged and interested in the learning you are planning.

Differentiation is often described as being achieved in one of two ways:

- through the *task* devised, by creating learning resources that suit differing abilities; or
- by *outcome*, by using the same resources for all students, who will then perform differently according to their abilities.

The learning activities you plan for your students will obviously be central to whether your lessons will broadly succeed, or not. Students have different abilities even within 'streamed' groups where it is often wrongly assumed that there is a large degree of congruity. In 'mixed ability' classes the ranges of abilities are usually more apparent. These differences must be considered in your planning and preparation. It is therefore worthwhile re-minding ourselves of the different abilities that may occur amongst any group of students and remembering that while some students are 'able' in one respect, they may lack ability in another.

Many teachers find difficulties in enabling students with dif-fering abilities to follow a common scheme of work at the same pace. On a day-to-day basis some students will inevitably com-plete all the tasks set before them, whilst others in the same classroom will struggle. The prospect of an ever-widening gap occurring between the 'achievers' and the 'laggards' is not ap-pealing – particularly as this will simply get worse from one lesson to the next if not addressed. OFSTED subject reports regularly highlight the lack of appropriate differentiation of tasks and activities according to students' abilities. They also note the lack of appropriate challenge, insufficient motivation and poor pacing of many lessons observed. The achievement of successful differentiation must be planned for. Professional judgement is required to ascertain what is both manageable and achievable within the context in which you are teaching. It is possible to state a series of considerations for planning for differentiation, including:

- establishing clear learning objectives and outcomes with respect to students' knowledge, understanding and skills;
- devising a variety of teaching and learning strategies, tasks and activities to differentiate the students' learning experiences;
- using a variety of teaching and learning resources;
- opportunities to vary the pace and depth of learning;
- different strategies to assess, feed back and target set for students.

(Battersby, 1995)

This can be encapsulated into a flow diagram, which forms a cycle based on the planning of both schemes of work and individual lessons (Figure 3.1).

The work of Howard Gardner (1983) is often cited when the abilities of students are considered. Briefly, Gardner believes that there are many sorts of intelligence, reflected in a range of abilities which may be more or less developed in each person. These abilities may be listed as:

- linguistic;
- logical/mathematical;
- musical;
- spatial;
- bodily kinesthetic;
- interpersonal;
- intrapersonal.

According to which subject(s) you teach you will be able to identify particular intelligences from the list above that are the focus for your discipline. It is worthwhile noting that education in Western society places importance, perhaps unduly for some students, on the development of the first two types of intelligence in Gardner's list – linguistic and logical/mathematical. This may mean that students do not have the

Planning

- Clear learning objectives, shared with pupils.
- The need to plan small achievable steps.
- Schemes of work that plan for revisiting.
- Schemes of work that have a full range of structured and open-ended tasks.
- Develop the model of core tasks with reinforcement and extension activities.
- Schemes of work with clear progression.

Teaching

- Using a wide range of activities and teaching styles.
- Clear instructions, explanations and expectations.
- An awareness that each student has unique abilities.
- The importance of the pace of the lesson.
- The need for balance of questioning techniques.
- The use of open-ended questions and enquiries.
- Flexibility of approach and response to students.
- Encourage a supportive classroom atmosphere.

Differentiation strategies

Resources

- The importance of clearly designed, uncluttered materials matched to students' abilities.
- Using texts of appropriate readability.
- Using materials that are free of ethnic and gender bias.
- The ease of access to learning resources.
- Classroom display that encourages learning and reflects high expectations.

Student needs

- Talking with teachers about their learning.
- Talking to each other about their learning.
- Sufficient repetition to consolidate their learning.
- Varied activities to match students' attention span.
- The use of student review to set realistic goals.
- Positive marking which points to improvement.

Figure 3.1 Suggested differentiation strategies

opportunities to fully develop other forms of intelligence that are important in life, or that if they have a natural aptitude within other types of intelligence these do not receive the same recognition as the first two.

Lesson planning should be varied enough to include a range of the abilities and intelligences listed. Particular subjects will not be able to develop all of these on a regular basis, but may incorporate some elements of each over time.

For many teachers the dominant model of teaching they carry into the classroom closely relates to how *they* were taught at school. As a teacher you are an example of a successful product of the education system – you are a graduate who has a strong command of your subject and a desire to replicate your enthusiasm for that subject within others. Many teachers therefore tend to equate their educational experience and the way in which they were taught with a model of good practice. This perception often needs to shift – for a major part of teaching involves working with students who do *not* have the same abilities and aptitudes for learning 'your' subject in the way you did. Your planning therefore has to take account of students who are very different from you, both in terms of their abilities and their motivation.

All students are individuals, with individual skills and abilities. It therefore follows that we should aim to plan, as far as possible, to differentiate our teaching and learning to accommodate these differences. Achieving appropriate differentiation is not easy – particularly as lesson planning has to take into account aims, objectives, teaching and learning methods, resources, environment, class management, assessment, etc., and *then* has to consider the fact that not all students learn in the same ways, are differently motivated and require 'tailored' approaches to learning. Planning therefore has to be done primarily on the 'class' level, but with consideration of the need for differentiation in the case of particular individuals. Getting to know your students as individuals is therefore an important first step.

It is worth remembering that when you plan your lessons with differentiation in mind, varying the teaching resources to be used is only one way of achieving learning tailored to the individual needs of students. Differentiation can also be achieved through:

- *Use of oral question and answer* – this is perhaps the most common form of differentiation, where teachers pose questions to the group that vary from those requiring simple recall responses to more advanced analytical or evaluative questions. Choosing who will answer such questions, to ensure high levels of success and motivation amongst individual students, is a process of differentiation. Phrasing 'difficult' questions in a supportive way for less able students can also involve an element of differentiation.
- *Use of a support teacher or teaching/learning assistant* – often the most pressing need for differentiation of materials and teaching approaches will be presented by those students who have special educational needs. Whilst it is up to you to plan suitable activities for such students, these needs may also be met by specialist support in the form of a support teacher or teaching/learning assistant. It is important to maximize the effectiveness of such support. This can only be achieved if you have an opportunity in the planning stage to sit down with the support teacher and talk through what you intend to do in the lesson, what you would like the students to do and whether these approaches are sensible with reference to the special needs within the group. All too often this essential element of planning is missing because of the pressures on your time and the fact that many support teachers are employed only for their periods of contact with students, or are not present in all the lessons you teach.

- *Use of assessment* – in the first few paragraphs of this section we discussed the use of differentiation by task and differentiation by outcome. In essence differentiation by outcome – where all students are given the same work and the difference is apparent in the quality of the work they produce – gives little 'support' to less able students. If one assesses such work for evidence of attainment in a summative fashion the less able students will rarely gain a sense of achievement and will lose motivation. However, if the assessment is more formative – that is, assessment *for* learning, rather than simply *of* learning – the effects can be more positive. Consider not only marking pieces of work on the knowledge, skills and understanding reflected within the students' work, but also on what you know of their abilities and previous levels of performance. Such ipsative assessment, which assesses the current performance of individual students on the basis of their previous achievements, can be more motivational for less able students. This differentiated approach enables the less able to see evidence of their own progression, despite the fact that their overall attainment levels may not be high. Similarly, this approach can provide a much needed impetus to more able students who you suspect of 'coasting' and not making their best efforts on their work. The analogy of the 'personal best' performance from athletics may be helpful here in encouraging all students towards achieving the best that they are capable of.
- *Use of preferred learning styles* – when planning your lessons it may be possible to predetermine tasks for individual students, for example when they are completing group-based tasks, so that students who have a particular preferred learning style get to complete work that they are 'good' at. Obviously this approach should not be used all the time, for students must develop a wide range of abilities through a variety of learning styles – it is unacceptable for some

students to always be given the 'drawing and colouring' tasks and others the 'writing' or 'speaking' tasks just because they find these activities straightforward!

As previously stated, successfully achieving differentiation within your groups is not straightforward. It is particularly difficult with a new class that you do not know well. In the first few lessons that you teach a new group you will find that much of the differentiation you undertake is done 'on your feet', often through oral question and answer sessions. More diverse forms of differentiation can be applied later, once you have got to know the individuals.

Gifted and talented

Planning the learning for the highest achieving students you teach – those sometimes labelled 'gifted and talented', 'high achievers' or 'more able' – is an aspect of differentiation that can prove difficult to achieve. It appears that many teachers assume that the main focus of their planning, where differentiation is concerned, should be on those who are less 'able' rather than on those who are gifted. This is perhaps understandable. Gifted students will, by definition, usually be able to complete the work we set relatively easily and in this sense meet our learning objectives established for the class as a whole. They tend to cause us little trouble and are therefore not the main focus for our attention. However, they also run the risk of not being stretched academically, facing little intellectual challenge and as a result getting bored and disillusioned by the education they receive. Merely planning to give such students 'more of the same' does not adequately address their needs! They will be sensitive to the fact that they are simply being given work to enable others to catch up, be aware that they are not being sufficiently challenged, and realize that in your subject they are not given opportunities to extend their thinking. None of us want students to come away from our teaching with the assumption that our subject is either 'boring', 'too easy' or 'not relevant'.

When planning for gifted and talented students we need to consider their main attributes. These may be that they are able to:

- understand difficult concepts clearly and apply this understanding to new situations to make new interpretations, develop hypotheses, reach conclusions and explore solutions;
- communicate effectively using both written and spoken word;
- reason, argue and think logically;
- manipulate abstract symbols and recognize patterns and sequences;
- enjoy using graphs, charts, maps, diagrams and other visual methods to present information;
- be confident and contribute effectively in less formal teaching situations;
- relate well to other people and show an ability to lead, manage and influence others;
- understand others' views, attitudes and feelings;
- have a more highly developed value system than most students of their age;
- have a wide ranging general knowledge;
- transfer knowledge from one subject to another;
- be creative and original in their thinking, frequently going beyond the obvious solution to a problem.

(adapted from QCA NC website
www.nc.uk.net/gt/geography/
(guidance on teaching the gifted and talented in geography))

The advice given about planning lessons for such students is to aim to increase the level of challenge they face. This can be achieved by planning lessons which:

- expect greater independence from the learner;
- increase the pace of the learning process;
- encourage metacognition and self-review;
- increase the proportion of higher order questions;
- widen the range of sources used by the learner;
- introduce texts of greater density and abstraction;
- demand greater precision in language;
- expect students to justify their answers;
- provide more opportunities to transform and apply new ideas;
- provide more open-ended, problem-solving tasks.

(adapted from DfES, 2002a)

It may not be feasible to challenge gifted students in every lesson. When planning your lessons it will be relatively straight-forward to think about offering more exacting questions orally – such as those that require elements of analysis, synthesis or evaluation – almost as a matter of course. Expectations of the answers gifted students can give should be high. Also, at the planning stage, you might place reminders to yourself about talking to gifted students individually during lessons, setting more individualized targets for them and seeking to extend their understanding. Some tasks could be more open ended – such as providing gifted students with raw data and asking them the best ways to analyse or display it, seeking their justifications for the approach they adopt. Other tasks, such as setting up extended writing as part of an enquiry or decision-making exercise, might challenge students to establish their own strategies for problem solving. Asking them to justify decisions, or to think of future scenarios, may also extend their thoughts. The development of a range of 'thinking skills' and the introduction of a variety of different reading matter might similarly help to challenge gifted students (see Ferretti, 2005). In our planning we may not be able to introduce 'extension' tasks into every lesson, however over the course of a scheme of work we can plan to introduce extended enquiries, decision-making exercises or open-ended tasks that require a more sophisticated approach and level of response from the student.

Planning for difficult classes

Differentiation is the term used when planning one's teaching to address variations in the abilities within classes, including the need to plan for students with special educational needs. Within the remit of differentiation attention should also be given to planning for difficult classes – where defiant, apathetic, or physically and verbally aggressive students are the main focus for the teacher's attention. Such classrooms are stressful and tiring, for the norms most teachers expect and accept are different here. As such they require a particular, and different, approach to planning.

Many teachers react to such classes by planning *less*. Their reasoning is that because 'nothing works' it is a waste of time and effort preparing much for such children. Experience tells them that the usual rules no longer apply – for example, that students will only misbehave if they have poor quality teaching, badly planned lessons or insufficiently stimulating activities. Blum (1998) captures the essence of such problematic classes when he states:

> They often behave badly when lessons *are* brilliantly planned because they prevent the teacher from starting properly; they often behave badly because they have poor skills in the subject areas they are asked to study (usually literacy and numeracy);

but, most importantly, they often behave badly because they have a very thin layer of motivation and a low level of concentration.

(p. 2)

Most teachers struggle with such classes. The main aim of the lessons they plan may not be closely related to the subject. For example, the focus for such lessons might start by trying to establish an ordered and calm environment, with the expectation that from this 'base' the pace of learning can pick up. Students have to understand that high expectations will be placed on them, demands will be made and challenges faced. Momentum, pace and rigour need to be established in the classroom. This is very easy to say, but very difficult to establish. The normal expectations we have of classes – that they will (mostly) turn up on time, with the correct equipment, stay in their seats, that they will be prepared to listen to the teacher and each other, not shout out and that they have some motivation to learn – cannot be assumed with such classes. In these situations Blum concludes:

The lesson has to be planned very carefully, and the behaviour of the students managed impeccably, before any useful class response can be exploited and purposely fed back into the lesson.

(p. 12)

4

Practicalities Before You Enter the Classroom

This section takes the teacher from the initial phase of lesson planning to the point of lesson delivery in the classroom. It covers a range of practical issues that need to be considered within lesson planning, but which are not necessarily formally recorded in the plan itself. The principles of resource planning and production, with particular reference to the creation of worksheets, are dealt with – as well as notions of 'perfect planning'. The section ends with a checklist of things to consider after your planning is complete, but before you enter the classroom. Finally, advice is given on how to maintain your records of lessons taught.

Part of the process of lesson planning often involves the creation of new teaching resources, customized to your needs. Many existing departmental resources will be used by you and other members of the department: however, it is important that you are confident in your abilities to plan and differentiate materials tailored to your specific approach to teaching and learning. These materials are often produced as some form of worksheet.

With the widespread use of computer technology in schools there is now little excuse for worksheets being produced that have poor presentation quality. No worksheet should be badly reproduced, thoughtlessly laid out or visually dull. It is up to you to set the standard for acceptable presentation of work within the classroom – you cannot expect students to produce work that is both of a high intellectual quality and neatly presented if you do not adhere to these principles yourself. With the possibility of downloading and incorporating images or data captured from the Internet, worksheets should be topical and interesting. Most importantly, the learning objectives that provide the foundations for the planned lesson should be clear to both teacher and students through the worksheet.

The main strength of worksheets as an educational resource is that they can provide, for a particular group of students, specific materials, data, case studies and activities not found in other resources such as textbooks. They can be differentiated to the needs of individuals within the class. They may also be designed to 'dovetail' with an existing resource – for example, as an additional stimulus or set of questions to be used alongside a picture in a textbook, or a newspaper article. One of the main advantages of the worksheet is that it can be 'taken home' and used for homework, whereas textbooks are rarely allowed to leave the school premises.

Figure 4.1 shows some thoughts on worksheet planning and construction. These ideas may also help you to review existing teaching materials within your department during the planning stage. You will see how closely they link back to some of the principles utilized both in the construction of schemes of work and in lesson planning.

Remember that although each lesson plan describes a discrete learning experience, it also lies within a deliberate sequence of teaching and learning. Lesson plans, when taken together in their pre-determined sequence, should deliver the scheme of work that has inspired their creation. It is therefore important for you to be able to hold this 'big picture' in your head as you teach – you should be confident that your sequence of lessons and the activities they contain are an appropriate way of meeting the aims of the scheme of work. The plans should therefore describe an overall course of learning, where you are just as aware of what is 'coming up' in future lessons as you are of

Purpose:
- What is the purpose of the worksheet?
- What are the learning objectives I want to cover?
- What specific subject knowledge, understanding and skills will the worksheet address (in the NC, GCSE or AS/A2 level)?

Planning:
- What resources/materials do I need to construct the worksheet? Where are these available (textbooks, Internet, CD ROM, newspapers, photographs, cartoons, etc.)? Are these resources up-to-date and free from bias?
- Do I have the technical ability to construct and reproduce the worksheets?
- What activities should be included to meet the 'Purpose' outlined above? How will these activities be differentiated according to the abilities of the students?
- How will student learning be assessed?

Presentation:
- What design do I want for the worksheet – portrait or landscape, font sizes and types, pictures, maps, cartoons, tables, diagrams, graphics, etc.? Will visual images reproduce clearly if the worksheet is to be photocopied?
- Is the text engaging and clearly sequenced for the students? Is the text readable and is the amount of technical vocabulary and use of jargon acceptable?
- What headings and labels do I need to include to identify where activities are, or where figures and tables can be found?
- Is there too much/not enough text?
- Should key words (and their definitions) be identified in bold type?

Use:
- How does the worksheet fit into the lesson plan and its stated learning objectives?
- How will I introduce the worksheets to the students? Do I want them to complete it all in the lesson? Are any activities for homework? Are there different sheets and/or activities for different students?

Evaluation:
- Did the worksheet help me achieve my learning objectives?
- Was the worksheet capable of providing differentiated learning for different abilities?
- Did the students find the worksheet interesting, motivating and stimulating to use?
- What might I change about the worksheet, or the way I used it, in future lessons?

Figure 4.1 Some principles for designing a worksheet

what has 'gone before'. This is the key to successfully achieving sustained continuity and progression.

Perfect planning for perfect lessons

It is worthwhile holding in your mind an image of what might be the (near) perfect lesson. This will inform the planning process.

What criteria should we state for such a lesson? A few ideas are listed. First, the lesson should be planned to be:

- purposeful;
- well structured;
- flexible;
- differentiated;
- varied, in terms of accommodating different learning styles;
- well resourced, with resources being used effectively;
- challenging;
- well paced, dynamic;
- expecting high standards of student achievement;
- creating a good learning atmosphere;
- capable of conveying a sense of achievement (for both learner and teacher).

Second, from the perspective of the learner the planned lesson should:

- be purposeful: the reasons for learning should be clear (often this learning would have a practical application);
- involve active learning (including problem solving);
- enable students to use thinking skills, initiative and imagination;
- be used to acquire knowledge, understanding and skills;

56

- be enjoyable and satisfying;
- establish good working routines, confidence and high standards;
- clearly indicate continuity and progression;
- be assessed, by both the teacher and the students, in a formative way;
- be able to extend or alter the students' ways of thinking.

This implies that:

- teachers should have clear objectives for their lessons;
- students should share these objectives and understand them;
- teachers should have secure subject knowledge;
- lessons should have appropriate content;
- activities should be well chosen to promote learning of the content;
- activities should engage, motivate and challenge students, enabling them to progress.

(adapted from Tolley *et al.*, 1996)

The amount of time you will have spent planning your first lessons is often frighteningly large. Beginning teachers usually feel very nervous, not only about the content and structure of the initial lesson plans they put together, but also about the amount of time they need to spend in the planning process. It is only human nature to calculate that if it has just taken you three hours to plan one lesson, then when you come to teach 34 lessons each week the planning process alone will take the equivalent of about two working weeks! Obviously this is an unsustainable situation; all you would be doing each day in such circumstances is planning lessons – with no time left either to deliver them, or indeed to do anything else! This simple calculation is thankfully flawed – many of your lessons will be 'repeated' with other groups, a process which requires existing plans to be only slightly modified. Not all lessons will require the same level of detailed planning, particularly those where the time-consuming creation of new resources is not necessary; also, as your professional competence and knowledge of particular groups increases the time spent in planning decreases.

All lesson plans should be practical working documents. They should be neither too long nor too detailed (one side of A4 should suffice), for if they are too lengthy and convoluted in style they will cease to be of use in the classroom. You should be able to refer to them quickly in the lesson and to pick up immediately where you are and what you have to do next. Clear, concise and workable documents are the basis of effective teaching. The 'perfect' lesson plan is simply an *aide memoire* reflecting the detailed thinking and planning you have previously put into making the lesson a successful learning experience for your students.

Lesson planning is a circular process, involving:

- knowing what has to be taught to particular groups from the scheme of work;
- having ideas about how you ideally will teach the lesson content and how the students will learn;
- considering what materials already exist for this purpose;
- planning and teaching;
- evaluating and using the experience gained to alter future plans and teaching strategies.

Beginning teachers often find it helpful to get professional advice on their lesson planning, particularly if the group they are about to teach is unfamiliar to them. In doing so it may be helpful to follow the following route:

1. Consult the scheme of work.

2. Find out what the students have done before (continuity and progression).
3. Find out about the group – records, watch them being taught, talk to previous teacher.
4. Draft a lesson plan based on the information above.
5. Discuss the plan with the group's previous teacher/mentor/head of department/NQT or other colleague.
6. Change the plan according to the advice you have been given – be clear about your learning objectives, process and expected outcomes.
7. Finalize the lesson plan. Produce/access teaching and learning materials. Attach copies of teaching materials, content notes, 'reminders', etc., to the plan.
8. Book any resources, equipment, materials that you need for the lesson.
9. Teach the lesson.
10. Evaluate the lesson.
11. Refocus your thoughts and targets for the group based on the evaluative evidence gained.

When you come to teach the scheme of work again you should be able to complete the circle by referring to the evaluations you have made first time around.

Think through the lesson you have planned before you actually teach it. Mentally 'walk through' what you intend to do in the classroom. Imagine yourself in the context of the particular classroom, the particular group of students, the particular resources and the particular time of day. What might you have forgotten? What do you have to remember? Often this mental process of practical planning helps the teacher to ensure that the lesson taught is not a sterile 'off-the-peg' experience, but something that is more lively and bespoke. The odd little errors and mistakes that might occur, which can escalate into bigger problems, can often be eradicated in this way.

Lesson Planning

Remember that not all groups respond in the same ways to the same activities. Beginning teachers soon discover that with some groups they can almost do whatever they like in terms of teaching style, methods and materials used. Such groups respond positively to virtually anything put in front of them and will often learn effectively even if the materials are weak or the teacher is not performing at their best. The obverse is more problematic; some groups appear not to respond to anything. All the teacher's best efforts and most imaginatively planned approaches to learning (which may have taken hours to put together) rarely elicit a positive learning response from the students. It may be frustrating, but the only way to succeed in this situation is to plan even more skilfully and carefully, rather than reacting as human nature sometimes dictates by not planning at all.

Immediately before entering a lesson armed with your lesson plan and teaching materials, it is worthwhile to run through a brief checklist to ensure that you will not fall at the first hurdle. Each of the factors below will have hopefully been considered previously, but it is helpful to pose yourself the following questions *just* before you teach:

1. Is the classroom laid out how I want it? You may not have the luxury of access to the room, or time to arrange things exactly how you want them, but at least think about how you might organize the class at the start of the lesson. This applies to the possibility of putting the learning objectives, diagrams, key questions or notes on the whiteboard beforehand, or having them prepared on an OHP transparency.
2. Do I have all the resources and equipment I need to hand? Think about how many students there are in this group and whether you have the right number (with one or two spares) of worksheets, textbooks, coloured pencils, etc., for the activities to succeed. Did you take the students' exercise books in

during the previous lesson? Particular attention should be paid to the availability and pre-booking of videos, computers/computer room, TV, etc. Do you know how to work all these pieces of technology? Will the students remember to bring *their* basic classroom equipment (pens, rulers, pencils, etc.)? If you have a group that regularly 'forgets' to bring these items you may need to lend them materials to enable you to get on with teaching a successful lesson.

3. What will I do if the activities I have devised take a longer/shorter time than I've planned for them? You may need to consider the need for extension activities or for the production of other differentiated materials for such eventualities. Even groups that are supposedly 'streamed' contain a wide range of different abilities and levels of motivation amongst the students. Not all students will be good (or weak) at the same things. Some students will work quickly and accurately on a task, others quickly and inaccurately; some will be slow, methodical and accurate, others will just be slow! Account must be taken of these differences within the activities you plan.

4. Will the lesson rely on the students bringing learning materials which I have previously asked them to prepare? If you plan your lesson around an activity where students have been asked to 'bring something in' – newspaper cuttings, information downloaded from the Internet, etc. – always have a few spare copies available. The lesson will be a complete non-starter if they have forgotten to do this!

You will soon be able to quickly appraise what is necessary to make your lesson planning and preparation a success. A quick glance at your plan before the lesson will remind you of any key points you need to remember – whether they relate to learning activities, resources or behaviour – and you will be able to judge whether what you have planned stands a good chance of succeeding. In a busy working day, where one lesson often follows on immediately from the last and where a new group of students is coming into your classroom as soon as the last group has left, you will not have time to pore over your carefully prepared plan before you have to teach it. This underlines the necessity of producing clear, well-structured and concise plans.

Be sure about your learning objectives, communicate these to the students and engage them in activities that are both educational and fun. The key to good teaching and effective learning is variety – don't become too predictable in what you plan! Establishing a rhythm for each lesson is also important. Don't talk or ask questions for too long, and similarly don't let the students undertake too many lengthy activities: there should be a healthy balance between teacher-led work and student-centred activity. Remember that 15 to 20 minutes of doing the same thing is a long time for many children (and adults!). Interestingly, recent initiatives such as the 'three part lesson', and some standardized approaches to planning introduced through the Key Stage 3 strategy (see Appendix 2), numeracy and literacy hours, may imply the use of a more rigid framework for planning and teaching lessons. These should not be allowed to dominate your planning to such an extent that your lessons become predictable and therefore ineffective.

The most important thing is that the impressive looking lesson plan you have taken time and effort to prepare actually translates to a set of sound learning experiences in the classroom. If the conception of the plan is wrong then however impressive it looks it will not help you to ensure that your students actually learn.

Finally, do not attempt to plan too many lessons before you have had a good opportunity to get to know the group you are teaching and their particular wants and needs. Well-intentioned efforts may be wasted by beginning teachers using their precious time planning a series of lessons for particular groups that they do not yet know well. Invariably these lesson plans all have to be radically altered later, as they are often 'pitched' at the wrong ability level, or contain learning activities ill-suited to the students. Once you have got into your stride of planning and teaching, check that you are making adequate progress against the overall plan laid down in the scheme of work: it would be embarrassing to finish your term's work having only covered the initial stages of the scheme, or conversely to find that you have done everything within the first few weeks of teaching!

Keeping a record

Always keep hold of your lesson plans after you have used them – it is important that you file this paperwork in an orderly fashion. Having expended a great deal of time and effort on planning suitable learning experiences you would be foolish to simply misplace or disregard the lesson plans you have created. The system you choose to store such plans is up to you. Some teachers keep their plans in files according to the year groups taught in the National Curriculum, with similar collections of plans for GCSE and AS/A2. Others place together all plans on a particular theme, or have differentiated plans with collections of materials for either 'high' or 'low' ability groups. You may choose to keep paper copies of your plans and resources, or store them electronically. Whichever approach you choose to adopt, aim to keep a consistent, ordered and well-structured system of plans. Nothing is more frustrating than having to 'reinvent the wheel' where lesson plans are concerned; however, you must look to update your plans each time you use them, otherwise you will find that as each year passes your teaching is getting more and more dated and irrelevant!

Many teachers will have embarrassing memories of starting to teach a particular group the same lesson that they taught them earlier in the week. This sounds like hopelessly poor organization and planning, but such fundamental errors do occur – particularly if you teach more than one class in a year group and each of these classes is following the same scheme of work. You must therefore have a short-term record of which lessons you have already taught to which groups and with which plans, otherwise you may find yourself in a similarly disconcerting position.

5

Wider Aspects of Lesson Planning: Making Your Lesson Plans Work in the Classroom

Planning and preparation are the foundations of good teaching. A well-planned lesson will anticipate potential difficulties, whether they are conceptual or behavioural, and will have contingencies ready to either avoid or surmount these problems. However, preparation will only take you so far – at times the unexpected and unpredictable will happen and no amount of planning will help you! Experienced teachers may have seen these situations before and almost intuitively know how to deal with them; they do not need to specifically plan for these events but are confident that they can deal with them by thinking 'on their feet' and acting appropriately. Beginning teachers do not generally have this expertise and therefore need to consider possible eventualities more fully, planning for them if they can.

The next section of the book will outline the practicalities involved in making your lesson plans work in the classroom. It focuses on factors that might either disrupt your carefully prepared plans, or divert students from your lesson objectives. Advice is given on aspects of classroom practice that either do not regularly feature in lesson plans, or which are sometimes merely assumed within the planning process.

Classroom management

It is not the purpose of this book to exhaustively detail aspects of classroom management for teachers: many excellent works already exist which take this as one of their major themes (Kyriacou, 1986, 1995; Cohen *et al.*, 1996; Capel *et al.*, 1999). However, without clear ideas and approaches to such management your carefully planned lessons will not succeed. Most of the techniques of class management are generic in that they apply equally to teachers of all subjects, although certain teaching situations in particular subjects are in some ways unique and require particular management techniques be applied. Examples of these would be conducting fieldwork, teaching 'practicals' in Science, or supervising the use of machinery and hand-held tools in technology-based lessons.

Nonetheless, it is worth stating some of the basic aspects of class management that most teachers need to consider when they plan and deliver their lessons. Although few teachers will actually note down *how* they are intending to manage their lesson, an understanding of this must underlie any lesson preparation.

Lesson beginnings

Achieving a successful start to a lesson is most important. It is the period when students decide whether they are being offered a valuable educational experience that they will engage with, or whether they will reluctantly endure the next 70 minutes! A variety of things convey an impression of whether the lesson will be useful (from the students' perspective) and to what extent you have the confidence and authority necessary to teach the lesson. You must therefore plan to do the following:

- If possible, arrive in the classroom before the start of the lesson. Put the aim of the lesson on the board, organize whatever teaching resources or technology you will use, check the classroom layout and make sure you have everything you need 'to hand'.

- Greet the students at the door, either line them up and organize an orderly entrance to the classroom or supervise their entry with reminders to sit down quickly, get coats off, take out exercise books, etc.

- When the majority of students are in the classroom settle them down, get them to look to the front (try to get eye contact and scan the classroom) and to put down any pens, pencils or books they may be distracted by. Try to ensure complete silence before you 'start' the lesson – expect it, ask for it, wait for it. Students must not be talking and should be listening. A register is often taken at this point, which also helps to establish control.

- Be clear about the aims of the lesson. Students perform best when they understand both the purpose of the lesson and your expectations of how they should act and perform (academically and behaviourally) within your classroom. Problems often occur if students are unclear about what they have to do, how they should do it and what will happen if they don't! Lessons should be given a context – what did you do last lesson? What are you going to do this lesson? What will this lead on to and why is this important in this particular subject?

- Try to learn and refer to students by name (a seating plan will help). Some names you will learn very quickly (perhaps for obvious reasons!) – class management is much easier once you can directly refer to an individual student by name rather than offering vague comments to a group of students.

- Be clear and concise when giving instructions about activities you want the students to undertake.

Much of the above might be described as being part of the everyday 'craft of the classroom' that most teachers use. Most of it will almost certainly not be featured in your lesson plan (except for the aims of the lesson and the learning objectives): however, the success of the lesson might be less assured if each of these factors has not been considered previously, during the lesson planning stage.

Starters

Getting a lesson under way in a brisk and purposeful fashion is extremely important. Establishing momentum early in the lesson is essential, both to capture student interest and then to maintain pace and challenge. You should aim to achieve a focus on the main theme of the lesson, but in such a way that the new learning of the students is placed into the context of what they have previously learnt. Prior knowledge can therefore be used to introduce a new theme.

Starters are often used to establish an interactive 'flying start' to the learning. They seek to involve all the students in the class and develop a range of thinking skills and motivations. As such they:

- are essentially active in nature;
- focus on an appropriately demanding pace in thinking and learning rather than on the business of the activity;
- provide thought-provoking and engaging beginnings to lessons;
- are not 'compulsory' but can add greatly to a lesson's effectiveness;
- can be used to create lively introductions and are the first stage in meeting the key lesson objectives;

- can include brief, small-group activities prior to whole class work;
- can be used for 'little and often' teaching of skills;
- can be planned as a sequence of discrete units to build knowledge, understanding and motivation over a series of lessons;
- exploit prime learning time – students are often at their most receptive at the beginnings of lessons and concentration levels are high, yet this is often devoted to administrative and organizational tasks.

(DfES/QCA, 2002)

Thinking about the purpose of employing starters listed above, consider how this will affect your lesson planning. In a brief plan you might only note down the word 'starter', a time allocation of (say) 5 minutes and an indication of the actual activity you are choosing to employ – however, the planning will perhaps have considered many of the points above.

A number of quick 'starters' could be used. Each of these should achieve a focus on the objectives of the lesson in a way that gains the students' attention and interest. It is important to vary the starters used so that the learning experience does not become too predictable and therefore potentially boring. Figure 5.1 lists and explains some starter techniques.

It must be remembered that the point of planning 'starters' is that they are just that – a start to a more major theme or set of activities that will follow on in the lesson. Although starters are often best planned for the beginning of the lesson they can be used at almost any point in the students' learning as a means of 'energizing' and refocusing their efforts. They can provide a variation from what often becomes a tired and repetitive routine of using 'question and answer' to recap a previous lesson, or a recently completed task.

There are some inherent difficulties with using starters. These will occur on occasions, but can be thought about

Lesson Planning

Technique	Features
Sequencing	Provide students with envelopes containing brief statements on cards on some aspect of the theme you are about to teach. The cards can then be formed into a logical sequence by the students. Students are asked to explain why they chose their particular order.
Card sort	Provide small groups of students with pairs of cards (on the theme you are about to teach) that can be setted into pairs. The groups of students work to see who can get the correct pairings quickest.
Continuum	Provide students with a 'line' that describes a continuum, starting and finishing with polar statements. The students then have to place themselves somewhere on the line. For example, the continuum might stretch from 'I believe that nuclear power is the only solution to our future energy needs' to 'I believe that only green, renewable sources of energy should be used in future'. This works well with aspects of affective, values-led education. Students can be asked to explain their choice of position on the line.
Traffic lights	Students are given a red, an amber and a green card. They can use these at selected points either to register their understanding of a concept (e.g. red means 'I don't understand', amber means 'I *think* I understand', green means 'I definitely understand'); or to show whether a statement a teacher makes is true (green), false (red) or whether they are not sure (amber).
Mini whiteboards	Teacher asks a question and students write an answer on their mini whiteboards – which are then held up so the teacher can gauge the levels of knowledge/understanding of the class.

'Five things'	Teacher asks for 'five things' (or whatever number seems most appropriate) that each student (or group of students, or class) can provide as statements on a particular theme. This is often useful as a means of recapping on prior learning. For example, the teacher might ask for 'five things that make a good site for a car assembly factory', or 'five things about effective defending against corner kicks', or 'five things about the character of Hamlet', or 'five things that were the causes of the First World War'.
Stimulus	Teacher shows something thought-provoking (a newspaper headline, a piece of art, a photograph, an artefact, a short demonstration) to gain a reaction or response from the students. Questions can be set around the stimulus.

Figure 5.1 Some starter techniques
(after Elliot, 2004)

beforehand to try to eliminate them at the lesson planning stage. The main problems encountered are that the starter:

1. takes too much time, 'drifts' into time put aside for other (more major) activities and consequently destroys the pace and direction of the lesson;
2. lacks any clear learning objective and is not closely related to the main theme of the lesson;
3. does not suit all abilities of students and is difficult to differentiate within a limited time frame;
4. becomes a routine and predictable activity;
5. is easily ruined by lack of focus, lack of pace, students arriving late or students not concentrating on the task set quickly enough.

It is therefore important to plan starters that all students feel they can engage with and make some contribution towards. This will be challenging if you are teaching a group with a wide mix of 'abilities', or students who have English as an additional language (EAL), or have special educational needs (SEN). However the key is to try to make starters establish the expectation that the students will have to *think* and *participate* in the lesson, at whatever level they can. It may also be important to add extra challenge for more able students, perhaps by extending into higher order thinking skills or making the activity more sophisticated. You must remember to be firm in adhering to planned timings; deal directly with distractions, misbehaviour and latecomers; and aim for variety. It is important when planning such activities that we create the right kinds of learning atmospheres for our lessons, where student interaction and involvement is not just hoped for but expected.

The main points when planning good starters are:

- plan a starter that meets the lesson objectives;
- plan an activity that will be brief and keep to your timings;
- make your instructions and questions clear and concise;
- deal with diversions and distractions decisively;
- try to differentiate to ensure that all the students can play a meaningful role in the starter activity;
- keep starters varied.

Transitions within lessons

The achievement of successful transitions within lessons, that is changing from one activity to another, has to be carefully planned and managed. These shifts in direction can disrupt the flow of a lesson if handled badly and could spoil the working atmosphere you have worked hard to create. With some groups you may be able to achieve such transitions seamlessly – by simply highlighting what you want the students to do next on a whiteboard, OHP transparency or worksheet and trusting well-motivated students to get on with it. With other classes, where differentiation and pace of working is more of an issue, you may wish to have short, achievable activities punctuated by explanations of each transition (and possibly reinforcing what has just been learnt and your rules of classroom behaviour at the same time!). Obviously it is risky to allow students who have completed an activity to be left waiting to be directed onto their next task. Such 'gaps' are invariably filled by students talking and hindering the learning of others!

- Once the lesson is underway and the students are (say) engaged in an activity, move around the classroom and support individuals/groups in their learning activities. The pace of the lesson should be brisk and purposeful, but not at the expense of less able students' learning. Scan the classroom the whole time to spot potential problems. Act confidently if problems occur – you do not have a lot of thinking time in many situations but will soon develop an ability to 'think on your feet' and predict where problems might arise (and how to cope with them). Although the formal planning process may not be able to take into account all eventualities in the classroom, there will almost certainly be some groups that you teach where you will know from previous experience that you will need to pre-plan what you will do in given situations.
- When you wish to change an activity, be clear about how students should carry out the new activity and how long it will take. Stop students working and get them to look towards you, with pens down and listening. Establish silence before you explain what you want the students to do. Do not be in too much of a hurry to move on – it is essential that students understand what they should do for the next x minutes and

how they should do it. It is often best to run through an 'example' with the whole class to check that they all understand what they have to do. You do not want to spend ages going around to individual students dealing with the same problems time and again because you failed to explain the task clearly enough to the whole class.

- Reinforce your classroom 'rules'. Be clear and consistent about procedures for giving out and taking back equipment, about when students are allowed to talk, about the levels of noise you will accept during discussion work, about moving around the classroom, etc. All of these 'rules' can be considered by you in the planning stage. If you are sensibly consistent and reasonable students will also learn these rules and adhere to them, although some groups will require more reminders than others!

- Use your voice to help maintain control and management. Don't shout. Always aim to have silence when you talk. Remind students of this. When teaching use the full range of your voice to make what you say interesting and stimulating to listen to – vary the tone, loudness, pitch, inflection and pace of speech to give it interest.

- While students are working move around the class. Offer help if you see problems occurring, monitor what is going on, move towards trouble spots, catch students doing the 'right thing' and praise them for it! Aim to be as positive as possible in your class management.

- When you think that the time you have given students to complete an activity has come to an end, scan the classroom. Consider whether a little more time is still needed to get the whole class (or a very substantial number of students) to the end of what they are doing. Be flexible, but consider whether your timings need to be altered for similar activities in future lesson plans. Do not let activities 'drag on': keep the pace of the lesson brisk.

Lesson endings

Be aware of the amount of time you will need to gather resources back in from the students. This is a particular issue if large numbers of resources are being used, if students are in groups, if furniture needs rearranging before the next lesson or if the students have been engaged in role plays. The end of the lesson should be slick and orderly.

- The lesson must have a complete and tangible ending, just as it has a definite beginning. The end of a lesson will probably encapsulate the students' views of their learning experience with you – ensure that they go away with a positive impression of what they have achieved and how they have worked. Yours is just one of a range of curricular experiences students have each day – you want them to think it is something special.
- Recap on the students' achievements, set homework and ensure students have recorded this. Inform the students of what they are leading on to in the next lesson. It is often a good idea to get the students to express what *they* think they have learnt – this can be a rather salutary experience at times, but it does give you immediate feedback on one level as to whether the lesson has been successful.
- Dismiss the students in an orderly manner – there should be no rushing, no fighting to get to the door first, no noisy disruption. The classroom should, of course, be left tidy for the next teacher.

Each of these bullet points has detailed practical aspects of classroom management. Some beginning teachers learn these skills the 'hard way', through experiencing a number of difficult situations and 'hard knocks' in the classroom and then reflecting on how they might have handled these situations better. Others will have more successfully pre-planned for such eventualities, entering the classroom forewarned and forearmed.

Plenaries

Plenaries are used as a way to bring students together to explore what has been learnt. They are therefore often used to conclude a lesson, although they can be employed at any point within the lesson to 'draw together' what the students know, understand and can do. There is plenty of evidence, both from research and inspections, that in order to be effective plenaries should be carefully planned and closely linked to the learning objectives of the lesson. Unplanned or spontaneous plenaries tend to be less successful.

Elliott describes the purposes of plenaries as follows:

- a chance to review what has been learnt so far, including progress against intended outcomes;
- a time to direct students to the next stage of learning (sign-posting);
- a time to help students reflect on what they have learnt;
- an opportunity for the teacher to make formative assessments, identify and explore misconceptions;
- an opportunity to draw the whole class together.

(Elliott, 2004, p. 70)

Plenaries are extremely important in allowing you to assess whether students are meeting your planned learning objectives. As such they act as formative assessment opportunities, highlighting not only what the students have learnt, but also pointing out to the students how they have learnt, and what the next steps in their learning might be. The plenary can therefore be used to provide a time for students to reflect on, and clarify, what they have achieved. They can thus help to both consolidate and extend student learning.

The plenary that is used to conclude a lesson is possibly the most important one in your lesson plan – but equally it is often the one that is least successfully delivered! There are a number of reasons for this. Often the plenary becomes the least active section of a lesson where the teacher either sums up for the class what they have done and (hopefully) learnt, or the main content of the lesson is replayed through teacher-led question and answer. In this way only a few students gain opportunities to discuss what they have learnt. Despite tight planning, and close attention to proposed timings, teachers often run out of time in lessons – this is usually due to unforeseen events, discussions or activities taking longer than expected, or class management issues taking up time. The best way to avoid this problem is to pay close attention to planning your timings for each lesson and to make the structure and content of the plenary a more major part of your lesson plan. If you spend time and effort organizing the questions, activities and focus for your plenary at the planning stage you are less likely to let it fall by the wayside when you teach. If problems persist give a student the task of timekeeper – reminding you when there are 10 minutes and then 5 minutes left of the lesson so that you can fit the plenary in!

When planning, aim to vary the routine of the plenary. As with any teaching, if you always do the same, increasingly pre-dictable things they are bound to become boring both for you and the students. Inject variety – don't always ask the same type of recall questions, don't always ask students to state 'three things they've learnt this lesson', don't always set a homework and then ask 'who can tell me . . .?'. Plenaries can be used to re-engage attention, to fix the very specific aims and objectives of the lesson, and to establish the next phase of learning. Again, planning is the key. Instead of just repeating the 'facts' learnt in the lesson, why not get students to apply their new learning to a different question or context? Or set small groups of students a task which uses what they have learnt? Getting students to try to articulate the key points or concepts of the lesson is always revealing! Remember when you are planning to make sure that near the start of the lesson, or the main learning activity, you tell your students that a plenary will follow and that they will be expected to contribute. By warning the students of their expected role they may engage with and think about the task more closely and consider their own learning – particularly if they know they may very well be called on to say something in front of their peers!

The following are a set of approaches to plenaries exemplified in the Key Stage 3 National Strategy:

- ask students to draw out the most important points, explaining why they are significant;
- ask students to think of consequences, implications, parallel issues, and exceptions;
- ask students to generalize from their own experience;
- ask students to apply their learning to a new context;
- give the main points and ask students to illustrate each one;
- ask students to explain the objective and how it can be achieved;
- ask students to devise golden rules or tips for others attempting the same task;
- ask students to write up their findings on the board, on posters, or in a PowerPoint presentation and then allow time to view, interrogate and/or prioritize;
- provide 'prior warning' about what the plenary will involve.

(DfES/QCA, 2002)

One of the most important points when ending a lesson is to ensure that students do not make their own decisions about when the lesson is over. Setting of homework, as recorded in your lesson plan, is often taken by students as a sign that the lesson is over. Similarly plenaries may not be taken seriously by students if they feel they are the last 'time filling' exercise employed by the teacher to soak up the last few minutes before the bell. Ensure that you plan to avoid this – make the plenaries purposeful and integral to the lesson, containing clearly articulated (and understood!) tasks for students to engage with.

In conclusion, the following are 12 keys to planning successful plenaries:

1. Plan for the plenary as a distinct element of the lesson but specifically designed to help deliver the lesson's key objectives.
2. Choose the type of plenary which best fits the lesson's purposes.
3. Ensure that students feel confident and expect that they will all contribute to the session.
4. Provide opportunities for students to review and clarify their learning.
5. Allow and encourage reflection on what has been learned and how.
6. Use varied strategies rather than a repeated routine (remember the kinaesthetic learners).
7. Extend students' feedback by probing and extending questioning – this is to avoid low-level reiteration.
8. Synthesize in order to be explicit about big concepts and to aid transferability.
9. View the plenary as a key means of delivering progress – make sure the plenary draws out the progress made in the current lesson and extends thinking further, particularly over a series of plenaries.
10. Develop students' strategies to organize and remember what they have learned.

11. Build up a 'meta language'; a language to help students talk about their thinking and learning in a way which helps them with future challenges.
12. Make sure the place of the plenary is secure (ensure time allocated is not swamped by other activity).

(DfES/QCA, 2002)

Planning a management routine

It is important to quickly establish a set management routine for the classroom that is understood and adhered to by all the students. However, the students you teach will be used to other teachers' standards concerning classroom behaviour and will be sophisticated in their understanding of what will be allowed in the classroom. It is important that students have clear ideas about what will happen if they behave in certain ways – consistency and fairness of teacher response in given situations is essential to establishing a routine. Students expect you to have rules about how they should work, when they are allowed to talk (and about what!), whether free movement is allowed around the classroom, how they enter and leave the classroom and about oral question and answer sessions. It is wise to observe how other teachers approach these routines and to make some decisions about what rules you plan to establish before you teach each group of children. This is as much a part of planning to teach as writing out formal lesson plans or deciding on your learning objectives.

Experienced teachers become well practiced in judging when teaching situations may become difficult to manage and when preventative action may be needed. Often they will act on an almost subconscious 'impulse' that has been sparked by particular types of behaviour being exhibited by certain students, or by an impression about the ways in which the whole group of students is working. This is, of course, difficult to quantify and hard to convey to the beginning teacher! It is similarly very hard to note down in lesson plans before the event. Anticipating problems and acting quickly and effectively to defuse them is a skill that develops with time – the unexpected *will* happen and may not always be susceptible to pre-planning.

Learning environments: planning classroom layout

Your lesson plan should consider the layout of every classroom you teach in. The classroom layout – indeed the general class-room environment – will effect how you teach, how the students react to your teaching and ultimately what is learnt. Students will not generally perform well if the environment in which they are taught is untidy, dull, disorganized and lacking in visual interest. The neatness, order and presentation of the learning environment is important. Display materials create a significant impact in this respect – therefore plan to display some of the students' work to show that it is valued and worthy of public recognition.

In some classrooms active learning may be difficult because of space restrictions, the way desks and chairs have to be arranged (or may be permanently fixed), or because you have problems getting sufficient access to the classroom before the lesson. If the classroom is 'yours' – that is, you teach in it for most of the time and have all your resources and materials 'to hand' – what you plan may be different to what you would plan to teach in an unfamiliar, or distant, classroom. This is where planning becomes even more of a necessity. Devising how you will teach exciting and stimulating lessons in what may be a poorly equipped learning environment that is not conducive to your preferred styles of teaching (or the students' preferred styles of learning) is challenging.

Lesson Planning

Remember that classroom layout will effect the ways in which students interact. Rows of desks that face the front tend to imply a teacher-centred model of teaching, where the main interaction is between individual students and the teacher. Students' faces will all be visible to the teacher, who can see whether they are talking or concentrating. In classrooms where students are grouped on tables in fours or fives, the implication is that more student-centred learning will take place. Now students will not all face the teacher and will have a greater opportunity to talk to each other. This is ideal for groupwork and active learning, but may create a classroom management situation that is less easy for the teacher to handle. The teacher should therefore plan which layout of the classroom best suits his or her teaching and learning style, the behaviour of the group and whether an 'active' or 'passive' lesson is required.

If a classroom you have been asked to teach in is new to you, part of your planning should involve a preliminary visit to the room to check on where things are and whether they work! It is not good practice to arrive just before the start of your lesson unsure of whether the blinds work, whether there is an OHP in the room, where the electric sockets are located and if a projector screen is available. The availability of each of these will fundamentally determine what you can plan to do in this room. It is no good assuming that all classrooms carry the same range of 'basic' resources: they do not! Remember, it is always advisable to check such things beforehand – even if it means visiting the classroom prior to the lesson to plug in the OHP and project your first transparency. This often reveals things that might have ruined your otherwise carefully planned lesson – such as the OHP does not work, there are no replacement bulbs/OHPs available, the transparency is not clearly visible to the entire classroom, the projector screen does not work, the blackout for the room is inadequate, etc. It is always worth checking beforehand.

Common problems

As previously explained, good teachers get used to 'expecting the unexpected' and being able to deal with situations calmly and in a confident manner. Various incidents will affect the delivery of your planned lesson, but many of these incidents will be predictable. The teacher is therefore able to consider what his or her response will be *before* the event. Dealing with problems in such a way that the learning of the whole class is not affected more than is absolutely necessary is a sign of effective class management. For all other unexpected or bizarre occurrences you will have to trust your reactions!

Below are a number of common problems that occur within classes and suggested responses for the beginning teacher.

Students who are not willing to get on with the work that has been planned

Calculated idleness can take numerous forms. Often students claim that they do not have a pen or pencil to write with, have forgotten their exercise book or file, do not have work from a previous lesson that is to be completed in this lesson, or simply do not settle into work.

In response, always have a supply of basic equipment to loan to students, but ensure that you know who the equipment has been loaned to and that you get it back at the end of the lesson. Persistent calculated idleness such as lack of equipment or forgetting exercise books should be punished, having warned the student beforehand of future sanctions if the idleness continues. In some cases it is advisable for you to keep the students' exercise book (if they have no homework) so they cannot lose it from this lesson to the next.

Lesson Planning

Students who complete the work that has been planned too quickly

Although not specifically a student-initiated disruption, the rapid completion of set work – leaving the teacher with a vacuum to fill in the second half of the lesson – can present problems. This issue is largely one of planning the timing for the lesson and its activities, although there may also be considerations as to whether the work that has been completed quickly has been finished to the standards you would wish.

Reflect on your lesson plan and reorientate your timings for similar groups who will attempt these activities. Also think about the instructions you give to students about how they should complete their work and the standards you expect. Is the work too easy? Should it be differentiated for certain students? Is the work the students have completed acceptable? Are the tasks 'pitched' at the right level for this group of students?

If a 'gap' appears in your lesson that you had not planned for there are some short-term methods by which it might be filled:

- Ask extension questions on the theme of the lesson to be answered orally and/or in written form.
- Revise the main theme of the lesson to check understandings; rely on the students to tell *you* rather than you repeating the lesson's content.
- Set the scene for the next lesson; reveal the continuity and progression in the theme for the students.
- Set up small discussion groups amongst the students on one or two key questions or concepts you have taught.
- Have a 'generic' worksheet (or extension questions) available for the particular unit of work, that can be used in any lesson.
- Ask students to devise questions on the theme. Use this as a way of finding out areas that the students are not yet fully

confident about and start the next lesson from where the students 'are at'.

- Discuss the homework they have been set for the lesson.

Students who do not have enough time to complete the work planned

Often if students feel that they have to complete tasks that are too challenging, either in terms of the amount of work they are asked to do in a given time or the intellectual demands of the work, they will lose motivation and become disruptive. This is a problem that is easily exacerbated by simply having too much work planned for a lesson and attempting to get through it all too quickly.

Essentially, it is within the teacher's professional judgement as to whether the work that has been planned for a lesson is either too great, or too demanding. It is wrong to 'undersell' a lesson – that is, making the activities too simple or unchallenging to ensure that both the teacher and students have a relatively easy time of the teaching and learning process. However, it should not be the case that every minute of the lesson is spent in an exhausting intellectual struggle and a race against the clock! Getting the balance right is important.

Sometimes the solution to the problem of planning too much work is very straigthforward – simply plan less work and have a more realistic, but honest, appraisal of what students are capable of doing within each lesson. It is a natural reaction to 'overplan' lessons at the start of one's career, through fear of running out of material.

From successful planning to successful teaching

Many teachers talk about a 'craft of the classroom' and the establishment of a teaching and learning 'rhythm' within each lesson. Successful teachers almost take this for granted – they have internalized what makes their own lessons work with different groups of students and may find it hard to describe exactly what they do to be effective in the classroom. Passing on this professional wisdom to other teachers is therefore problematic. Incorporating it within lesson planning may be even more so.

Nonetheless, successful lessons tend to have components that can be planned. These include:

- 'Grading' the difficulty of the tasks, and the thinking, that students have to undertake. Experienced teachers suggest that successful lessons may start with some easy activities – such as the students listening to a brief recap of their previous learning, or responding to a small set of closed recall questions – followed by harder activities such as students responding to open questions, understanding reasoning tasks, and engaging in decision making. By planning to 'hook' the students into the new phase of learning early in the lesson, and by grading each educational step within the lesson from 'easy' to 'hard', the teacher has every opportunity of supporting the students along the educational pathway that has been planned.
- Establishing a 'rhythm' within the lesson. There should be periods of contrast within each lesson, rather than merely doing the same thing for long periods of time. Thus each lesson should have planned episodes of student noise and activity, followed by opportunities for quiet calm and contemplation. To ensure effective learning you don't want to have too much of one or the other – accentuate the difference between them.
- Leaving time for a meaningful plenary. Lessons that are planned to consist entirely of activities, with no time for reflection, are invariably not the most successful at advancing

student learning. You should plan to have time at various points in the lesson, and almost certainly at the end, to allow students to reflect on what they have learnt. This time has to be structured carefully by the teacher. It is wasteful to conduct lessons that appear to be successful on the surface, but which simply engage students in 'busy work' that they may enjoy but which has not taught them anything. Plenary sessions are therefore vital for the teacher because they reflect what has been understood by the students.

- Achieving a positive ending to the lesson. Good lessons should always finish with a well-rounded and purposeful ending, rather than fizzling out or ending with a poorly managed collection of resources, or hurried homework setting. It is very important to end in a structured and evenly paced fashion. This is the last memory of the lesson taught for both you and the students – make sure that the lasting impression is strong. Time should be planned for praise, a recap of key points, and for a look forward to the next lesson. Students should be reminded of the progress they are making in the short and long terms.

The points above highlight some practical ideas for turning your successful lesson planning into successful teaching. These focus on the planning of single lessons – however, it is important to consider what effect the act of planning lessons over an extended period of time will have on you as a teacher. All teachers get tired and stressed as the days, weeks, terms, and years progress. To be successful you will need to plan not only for the individual lessons you teach, but also for how these lessons combine over longer periods of time. Just as each lesson has a particular rhythm, so too does each week of lessons. Starting the new academic year with a flurry of exhausting activities for both you and your students may be well intentioned, with the aim of creating a good impression of yourself and the subject you teach, but is almost certainly unsustainable. Neither the students nor your fellow teachers will thank you if you are physically and emotionally spent after the first three weeks of term, with another twelve to go!

Pace yourself. Plan on storing some of your reserves, so that you can finish the term as effectively as you started it. Consider which are the essential tasks and which are merely time- and effort-sapping 'window dressing'. Make sure that you plan your working week so that not all of your 'active' lessons fall on one day. Ensure that each group you teach gets a mixture and variety of different types of lessons that are spread throughout the weeks that you teach them. Each day should involve some lessons that are more student-centred and some that are more teacher-centred. Do not plan to have days when you will be required to talk intensively to each class for each lesson – many teachers suffer from vocal strain early within the term and can, in extreme cases, do lasting damage to their voices. Beware the dangers of over-planning, seek to conserve energy, and beware of over-tiredness. Many of these things can be eliminated, or at least reduced, by effective short- and long-term planning.

Planning to be a good teacher

The question of what makes a good teacher is an interesting one. Although we have stated that planning and preparation are the keys to effective teaching they are not necessarily the sole de-terminants of being a good teacher. This can be frustrating – we all know of teachers who appear to be able to 'wing it' and still have an audience of children captivated by their every word!

It is worthwhile spending a little time considering different 'types' of teacher and seeing to what extent planning plays a role in their effectiveness. This is a useful exercise if you are able to honestly evaluate your own teaching persona, or have help from a mentor or colleague who will be critically supportive about how they (and the children) see you as a teacher. Information of this sort, although sometimes difficult to accept, will help you to concentrate on what is necessary to increase your educational impact and even extend your job satisfaction.

Moore (2000) highlights three 'models' of good teaching – the charismatic model, the competence model and the reflective model. He suggests that most teachers possess elements of each of these and that the adoption of just one approach will not be suitable to become a really good teacher. When asked to describe the qualities of a good teacher most students will focus on surface personal qualities such as 'sense of humour', 'ability to communicate', 'good at discipline', 'enthusiastic about their subject', and 'fair'. However, the less immediately obvious qualities that most good teachers possess – such as those to do with planning, preparation, organization, administrative strength, assessment – tend to be forgotten or to be considered of secondary importance by students. In essence, what is remembered is the 'teacher as personality' – and those teachers with the biggest personalities are those which often get labelled as 'charismatic' teachers. Moore (2000) characterizes such teachers as achieving success often in unconventional ways: 'in ways that have little to do with such mundane matters as planning and preparing for lessons. On the contrary, the charismatic teacher is often described as coming into the classroom deliberately *un*prepared – solely reliant on his or her subject knowledge, inherent popularity, and intangible ability to enthuse and inspire students' (pp. 120–1).

This approach can be very attractive to beginning teachers, but is extremely difficult to emulate. Such teachers may be the strongest influence on the training and induction of beginning teachers, and will almost certainly be the ones they remember from their own school days – but they are a hard act to follow.

Also, by downplaying the need to plan and prepare, they can send a potentially disastrous message to teachers who try to copy their approach to teaching. A more helpful 'model' to try to adopt is perhaps that of the teacher who is an effective *communicator*, rather than being overly charismatic. Both types of teacher will have strong personalities, but the communicative teacher 'is sensitive to the range of needs in the classroom and works and plans effective communication strategies both before lessons (in the planning stage) and after lessons (in the evaluative stage)' (Moore, 2000, pp. 121–2). Such teachers often *appear* charismatic to students, but are in effect actually good communicators who plan and prepare carefully and understand the importance of enthusiasm, understanding and performance in the teaching and learning process.

The competence model of effective teaching has much to do with the discrete *skills* that such teachers possess. Moore frames his description of these teachers in the context of competency and standards based initial teacher training, where new teachers have been called upon to demonstrate a range of skills and abilities before they can be assessed as being competent to teach. Such systems recognize that effective teachers are not made up of a sum of competences, but that these provide the foundations to effectiveness inside and beyond the classroom. As Moore (2000) reminds us:

> Teachers do, of course, need to have sufficient subject knowledge to teach the students effectively, and they do, of course, need to be effective planners and classroom managers. Indeed a high level of personal organization and preparedness is generally agreed to be one of the principal requirements of good teaching.
>
> (p. 124)

The reflective practitioner model is somewhat different in that it does not necessarily focus on the acquisition of particular skills and competences, but on the ability of the teacher to critically reflect upon and analyse his or her experience in the classroom. As a result of such reflection the teacher then recognizes the appropriate skills, knowledge and understanding that have to be developed to become a more effective teacher and sets about changing things in order to achieve greater success. This obviously has a clear link to planning and preparation, which should take account of the reflections and evaluations the teacher has made.

Lesson plans on the Internet

Many teachers now search for teaching resources on the Internet. This is understandable in an increasingly technological age and can mean that one's planning for the classroom is conducted in a time efficient way. Internet sources have the advantage of providing teachers with topical information, including a vast array of textual, visual and statistical information that can be included in their lessons. There are, of course, caveats to the use of such material – often web based materials are biased and unreliable, the product of particular interest groups who have a specific purpose in putting information onto the Internet. There is a vast range of material available, but this is not regulated, governed, vetted or censored. Not all sources of information are free and some are too complex to be simply transferred into worksheets or interactive displays for particular age and ability groups. In short, teachers must have a keen awareness that web based resources – like any materials used in the classroom – must be handled carefully.

Discussing exactly how information from the Internet can be downloaded into worksheets or used in PowerPoint demonstrations and interactive lessons is beyond the scope of this book. However, it is worthwhile and relevant to consider the merits – or otherwise – of using 'ready made' lesson plans that are now available from the Internet.

The quality of web based lesson plans

Type 'lesson plan' into any search engine and you will be rewarded with a huge number of 'hits'. Many of the websites now dedicated to providing teachers with 'off the shelf' plans need to be treated with caution. When considering whether you should use any of these plans it is worth asking yourself three fundamental questions:

1. Who wrote this plan(s)?
2. For what purpose?
3. Will the materials/tasks/activities/concepts in this plan suit the students/curriculum I teach?

Many of the websites offering lesson plans are American and were designed specifically for the education system and state-based curricula of the United States. The quality of such plans is hugely variable – they are often heralded as being 'written by teachers for teachers', but merely serve to indicate that many practising teachers are not particularly adept at writing plans that either stimulate learning or are useful to others in the profession! Like any educational resources that are free and easily available to the teacher, web based lesson plans must be treated with a large degree of circumspection. It is worthwhile asking the same questions one would apply when designing worksheets (see Figure 4.1 on page 55 'Some principles for designing a worksheet') when considering whether or not to use such plans.

At worst the material can be heavily biased, prejudiced or even racist.

Strengths	Weaknesses
• An infinite number of resources and quantity of information – distance no object. • A two-way communication at little expense. • Developing rapidly into multimedia. • International information, mainly in English. • Constantly updated. • In digital format, so can be easily edited and 're-purposed'. • Hypertext format. • Encourages links to other sources making connections between ideas. • Information is free. • Spontaneous, innovative, knows no national boundaries, ungovernable, untameable, unstoppable.	• No framework or format – a jumble – no central catalogue. • Can be hard to find what you want – and too easy to be distracted to find things you don't want. • Encourages browsing rather than serious searching or reading. • Resources of variable quality, no vetting, no editing, no quality control. • Slow to load graphics, movies, sounds. • Difficult to censor unsuitable material. • Contains bias, prejudice and error. • Spontaneous, innovative, knows no national boundaries, ungovernable, untameable, unstoppable.

Figure 5.2 The Internet's strengths and weaknesses
(from Grey, 2001, p. 34)

When searching the Internet, either for material to be used in lessons or for 'ready made' lesson plans, it is worthwhile considering the strengths and weaknesses of the Internet listed in Figure 5.2.

Lesson Planning

Even if the lesson plans have been devised to 'fit' the curriculum or syllabus that you are teaching they may not be suitable for the children you teach, or the context in which you work. The best way forward is usually to scan such plans for ideas and activities – but to leave the actual lesson planning to someone who fully understands the educational context in which the lesson will have to be delivered. That is, you!

As this section deals specifically with accessing prepared lesson plans from the Internet, there is not the scope to discuss the use of the Internet in lessons, or teaching with ICT in depth. However, as the use of technology is increasing dramatically in lessons – particularly as schools become equipped with electronic whiteboards in a number of their classrooms – it is important to mention the implications when planning to employ ICT hardware in lesons. ICT has the advantage of bringing a wide range of topical, colourful and data rich sources of information into the learning process. It can be used to manipulate, edit and re-form text and data, while also helping students to improve the presentation of their work. It can speed up the creation of graphs, diagrams and maps. It can increase opportunities for communication and collaboration, while allowing more time for discussion, analysis and more autonomous learning. Nonetheless, fundamental questions must be asked by the teacher when planning a lesson using ICT:

- Will ICT be used in my lesson to further knowledge, understanding, or skills?
- Will it be used both as a tool and an information resource?
- Will it be incorporated effectively into the students' learning?
- Are the expected learning outcomes appropriate? Is the use of ICT the best way to advance these learning outcomes?
- Is the teaching strategy that is planned the best one for the learner?

As with any lesson planning we have to think about what advantages the use of ICT (like any other technique, methods or materials) actually brings. ICT is not a simple panacea for engaging 'difficult' children and can be used in very traditional ways. In our planning we must try to avoid the equivalent of electronic 'chalk and talk' lessons, or 'PowerPointless' presentations.

6

Lesson Evaluation

Evaluation is an essential tool in the process of learning to teach and helps you to understand and solve problems faced within the classroom. A lesson evaluation is not merely a *descriptive* account of class management or of events that happened in the lesson: rather it is a means of *analysing/problem solving* the ways forward for future teaching and learning. All aspects of the lesson planned and taught should be evaluated (including the content of the lesson) and improvements sought through the establishment of a set of constructive targets. Lesson evaluation is central to any teacher's professional development. The easiest way to think about the whole process of teaching is to imagine it as a cycle that starts with 'planning', then moves to 'doing', and then to 'reviewing'. This plan, do and review cycle continues from one lesson to the next – an evaluative feedback loop which constantly helps you both to reflect and look forward in your attempts to produce ever-improving learning experiences.

You should have a good idea of what constitutes having taught a 'successful lesson'. What do we mean by 'success' in this context? Does this coincide with the professional judgements of others? You may be happy with what you have taught and what you think the students have learnt, but would this judgement be the same if it were made by an Ofsted inspector, an induction tutor, or a member of the Senior Management Team of the school? The key to effective lesson evaluation (on whatever aspect of the lesson being evaluated) is professional judgement – a judgement that other professionals would make according to agreed standards. However, getting professionals to agree on such standards is problematic! Most beginning teachers naturally start to evaluate lessons in terms of their own performance as teachers, rather than of what their students have learnt. This is only human nature – we all want to know how well we have performed. Nevertheless, the essential element of evaluation should focus on what the students have learnt and whether we can be reasonably certain of the extent of this learning.

The overall aim of a lesson evaluation is to determine what went well, what went badly, how much the students have learnt and what you need to target for the future. To do this you need evidence. A very helpful source of evidence is gained through being observed by another teacher: however, because opportunities for structured observations rarely happen you need to become good at honestly evaluating your own performance. This is the essence of being a reflective practitioner, using the evidence of your own performance to determine how your lessons (and lesson plans) should change in the future (Figure 6.1).

On some lesson plans you may wish to detail wider aspects of the students' education that you seek to promote *through* the subject being taught. For example, this might include a particular aspect of literacy or numeracy, PSHE, citizenship or a cross curricular theme.

Evaluations and reflections on your lessons can work on a number of levels. Evaluation may be linked back to the original learning objectives stated on your lesson plan. If these learning objectives have been clearly defined the evaluation should be relatively straightforward. Some argue that evaluation can take place into all aspects of the lesson planned, or undertaken against set criteria devised at the time of planning. It is possible to use a variety of sources of evidence, such as the assessed work of the students taught. Reflection is often seen as being a more finely layered process – it involves the teacher analysing a

1. Aims and objectives	• Were the aims/objectives of your lesson wholly or partly achieved? • Did you manage to cover the content of the lesson? • Could students understand and use the subject knowledge/skills you introduced? • What do you think they actually learnt? • What did any assessment show?
2. Methods	• Did you have success with the various methods used? • Question and answer technique. • Visuals and OHP. • ICT. • Pair work, group work. • Games, role plays, simulations. • Practicals. • Differentiation. • Teacher-led sessions.
3. Management	• Was the start and finish of the lesson orderly? • Was the change of activities orderly? • Were students organized into effective learning groups? • Were instructions clear? • Were interruptions dealt with effectively? • Was a good learning atmosphere created? • Was the preparation of resources sufficient?
4. Control and discipline	• Type and use of reward/praise (smile, look, encouragement). • Type and use of censure (look, talk, action). • Tone and approach adopted towards class and individuals.
5. Resources	• Use of boards, textbooks, worksheets, OHP, ICT. • Were resources used effectively?
6. Follow up	• What should be planned next? • Should the content be covered again in a different way? Or should you teach something new? • Marking of books and feedback. • Specific targets for next lesson.

Figure 6.1 A framework for lesson evaluations

breadth of evidence, some of which may have been provided through evaluation, and then making decisions about future practice. The point is that reflection can help you make sense of whatever may have happened in the classroom and, most importantly, provide you with well-reasoned and professional 'ways forward' for future lesson planning. This explains the use of the term 'critical reflection', in the sense that such reflection is analytical, discerning, intelligent, thoughtful and probing.

Having just taught a lesson your reflections will almost certainly be instinctive and personal. When you walk away from a lesson that you felt 'went well' or 'went badly', for whatever reasons, you inevitably experience one type of rather emotive reflection on the process of teaching and learning. All teachers will experience this kind of 'first order' response to having taught a lesson. However, the more important reflective process is that which comes later through the types of critical reflection outlined above. It is all too easy in teaching to make hasty, and often inaccurate, judgements about your teaching and students' learning. Measured and professional reflection focused on specific incidents and outcomes is the key to making progress in your teaching. This relates to being able to 'step back' from the lesson you have taught and analyse what went well or badly and, more importantly, why this was the case. The next step is the most significant: deciding how you might improve the learning of the students in your classes.

Getting support for your lesson evaluation

All teachers can benefit from good quality feedback from an experienced observer. Such observation can help you to 'see' things that you can easily miss during the hectic activity of daily teaching. Another person's perspective and advice can be hugely beneficial to your development. Importantly, this 'critical friend' should be exactly what this term implies – someone who is capable of being constructively critical of your performance, but is also capable of being 'friendly' in the ways in which such comments are delivered. Evaluative comments must be skillfully handled and delivered if one is to ensure that the progress made is not abruptly stopped, or even reversed. Be careful about who you ask to observe you and seek to understand their perspective on observation – what you will be told about your teaching by a trainee teacher, a mentor, a NQT, other subject teachers, your head of department or a member of the SMT will be different. Each will bring a certain focus and level of formality to the observation process.

Lesson observations should be linked to the lesson plan. Perhaps the most effective way to benefit from an observation, if time allows, is to sit down with the observer before the lesson and discuss what the focus of the observation will be. The lesson plan should be central to this discussion. A variety of options are then apparent. Observation may involve:

- the observer noting general comments about whatever he or she wishes, whilst watching the lesson;
- the observer and teacher discussing what the focus for the observation should be (either the observer's choice, the teacher's choice or a mutual decision), followed by the observer watching the lesson;
- the observer only watching specific elements of the lesson, e.g. the beginning, the ending, transitions;
- the observer initially discarding the lesson plan and writing what he/she believes the lesson plan *should* be having watched the lesson.

Most important is the debrief at the end of the lesson. Again the lesson plan should be a focus for the debrief – were the learning objectives met? Were the timings accurate? Were the teaching methods appropriate?, etc. The conversation between the observer and teacher should obviously be handled sensitively. Both will need to remind themselves of the purpose of the observation and be aware of the criteria that were established for the observation. The aim is for a balanced, critical and professional conversation which seeks to improve the teaching of the person observed. Target setting is usually a feature of such a critically reflective discussion.

7

Conclusion

Lesson planning and effective preparation for the classroom are essential. The time that you can expect to spend on each of these, especially as a beginning teacher, will be very significant. As a result these activities may become stressful and prone to being rushed. If this is the case there is a tendency for negative feedback to occur – lack of planning leads to unsatisfactory teaching and learning experiences in the classroom, which results in teacher and student frustration, lack of motivation and general dissatisfaction. It is a sobering experience to calculate exactly how much time you spend outside the classroom on lesson planning (as well as on other essential activities such as marking, report writing, etc.) compared to the amount of time you spend actually teaching. Much of the time spent on lesson planning will also be 'off site': at home, usually at the end of an already long and stressful day. Nonetheless, planning can not be sidelined because it is central to successful teaching.

Some teachers are clear and effective planners from the start, others need more support and guidance. It is advisable to see the lessons you are planning as a sequence rather than as 'one off' events. The danger of the latter approach is that aspects of continuity and progression become submerged in the desire to teach a particular lesson, rather than a series of lessons.

Experienced teachers tend to be flexible in their approaches to both planning and teaching – they almost intuitively know what will 'work' with particular students and are efficient in the use of their precious planning time. This often extends into the classroom where such teachers are prepared to respond 'on their feet' to the various signals given out by students, altering their approach from what they have previously planned as situations dictate. Initially many teachers may not recognize the signs and the range of options open to them; even when they do, they may be overwhelmed by their apparent choices within any given situation. Planning for flexibility is difficult for teachers, many of whom will tend towards under-planning to achieve adaptability, whereas in fact the opposite is necessary! It is worthwhile thinking during the planning phase of the different teaching and learning approaches that might be used to achieve transmission of the same subject content. This helps to introduce versatility and flexibility into the planning process.

The time spent lesson planning must be skillfully incorporated into the overall time devoted to the job. You must ensure that you have an organized system, almost a timetable, for lesson planning that means that you do not have a planning crisis which regularly occurs each week on a particular day. Always finding yourself frantically planning last thing on a Sunday night is neither pleasant nor advisable. Individual lesson planning should not take up inordinate amounts of time, nor should you be so fatigued from evenings spent assiduously planning that you have no energy left for the classroom performance. In an already stressful job the addition of further frustration brought about by poor time management must be avoided.

Planning is a very significant aspect of your work. One of the major challenges of effective lesson planning is that the teacher has to prepare and deliver learning activities that closely match the needs of the students within the class. These activities have to promote various aspects of knowledge, understanding and skills within the context of the subject taught, as well as maintaining the interest and motivation of the learner. The lesson plan must take account not only of previous learning, but also of the students' readiness or preparedness to accept new learning. It must also be cogniscant of future learning requirements. All this has to be done in a challenging and fun way – whatever the content of the lesson, the time of day it is taught, or indeed whether the lesson occurs at the start, middle or end of a term or academic year.

Teaching is a very personal activity – it therefore follows that lesson planning to suit your particular teaching style and aptitude is also personal. However, there are fundamental principles and practices that largely define good teaching and good planning, as outlined within the earlier sections of this book. It is worth remembering that the same subject content can be successfully taught and learnt in a variety of ways and that there is no single successful style of teaching that can be planned for all learning situations.

Lesson planning brings together two types of knowledge, understanding and skill within the teacher. First, that which is associated with your professional competence as a classroom practitioner – that is, your ability to know what students are capable of learning, how they should be taught to meet these capabilities, and what types of activities should be planned and employed. This is sometimes called 'pedagogic' knowledge, understanding and skill. Second, that which is associated with your appreciation of your subject discipline and your competence as a biologist, mathematican, geographer, etc. When professional competence and appreciation of your subject discipline are combined in the effective planning of lessons this is sometimes referred to as utilizing 'pedagogic subject knowledge' (see Shulman, 1999). In essence, this is the knowledge of how to best teach the content and concepts of your subject.

Managing and organizing classrooms is rarely straightforward. These are the activities that most teachers are nervous of when they begin teaching – 'Will I be able to control the class?' In by far the majority of cases beginning teachers *do* achieve the necessary skills and techniques to manage classes within the early stages of their careers. This is not to say that once learnt these skills merely have to be applied in the same way to every class to be successful; many experienced teachers still face challenges and new demands within the classroom on a daily basis. Good management is clearly achieved through sound preparation and lesson planning. Fundamentally, the teacher is always attempting to reduce the number of 'unknown variables' that might occur within his or her lesson – and if the lesson is well planned and 'tight' these variables are greatly reduced. Therefore, if something untoward occurs, such as an unexpected confrontation with a student, the teacher can give this incident their full attention safe in the knowledge that other aspects of the lesson (the learning activities, resources, timing, assessment) are already carefully planned and running smoothly.

This book started with a description of a successful lesson. For the beginning teacher success is often built upon confidence in the classroom, confidence that is sustained from the knowledge that you enter the classroom with a well-thought-through, practical and workable lesson plan. It also requires determination, stamina, inventiveness and enthusiasm. Lesson plans should be dynamic, lively, working documents with a strong practical purpose – they are not merely dry, academic records of what should be taught.

Trying to distil the key elements of good lesson plans into a series of bullet points is not easy. Nonetheless the training materials for the Key Stage 3 Strategy on planning lessons conclude with a helpful attempt, reproduced below.

Good lesson plans are brief but usually have:

- lesson objectives which can be shared with students;
- a clear structure for the lesson;
- brief notes on key questions and teaching points;
- brief notes on specific activities;

- brief notes relating to needs of individuals or groups (for example, SEN or G and T);
- a note of how any additional support will be used;
- reference to subject issues, for example developing vocabulary;
- references to relevant resources;
- an indication of any homework to be set.

What is clear is that the majority of students respond positively to the effort made by their teachers to plan and prepare lessons. The time and care that teachers take in planning has a directly beneficial effect on what occurs inside the classroom. Students appreciate that the learning activities and materials planned have their educational interest at heart, particularly if they also prove to be entertaining and fun! However, the reverse is also true – students will be insulted if the teacher does not bother to plan his or her lessons effectively, and will often respond by giving such lessons little attention.

Exemplar Lesson Plans

This section comprises examples of completed Lesson Plans for a range of National Curriculum subjects.

I extend my thanks to Clare Hipwell (History), Jonny Mellor (RE), Katie Underwood (PE), Catherine Owen (Geography), Kelly Pearson (MFL) and Raksana Bibi (English), who were all trainees on the University of Birmingham PGCE course 2004–5, for providing examples of their lesson plans for use in this section.

These Lesson Plans vary both in the formats they adopt and the level of detail they convey. Some are detailed to the extent of being almost a 'script' for the lesson (see MFL), while others also include an evaluation of the lesson taught (see RE and English).

Lesson Planning

HISTORY

Class: 7y2n **NOR:** 25 **M:** 16 **F:** 9 **Ability:** Lower Middle

Time: 60 minutes

No. on SEN register: 6

Unit of Study: The Roman Empire

Context [Previous Work/Next Work]:

Previous – Who murdered Julius Caesar?

Next – The Roman army

Learning Objectives/Outcomes: To investigate – Why was the Roman army so successful?

Most students will be able to describe the reasons for the success of the Roman army, use source material to explain the organization, training and weapons used by the Roman military.

Some students will not have progressed as rapidly and will be able to identify weapons and armour used by the Romans, be able to suggest reasons for the military success and use source material to provide basic descriptions of Roman training, weapons and organization.

Some students will have progressed further and will be able to use a range of source material to analyse the reasons for the military successes of the Roman army, suggest limitations of the Roman army, they may be able to offer more than one interpretation of why the Romans were so successful. Choose which area – training, weapons or organization – was the most important and support this with evidence from the sources.

Skills:
Evaluation
Enquiry
Interpretation
Analysis (use of historical evidence)
Develop use of new technique for accessing, evaluating and differentiating information – Venn diagram
Some students will have learned how to analyse, synthesize and apply this information to the key questions

Language for Learning:
Subject specific vocabulary: legion, century, centurion, auxilia, aquilifer, signifier, legatus, sword, shield, armour, tortoise, catapult

General vocabulary: successful, organization, discipline, formation

Language experience:
Listening: To the teacher and each other
Talking: Paired and class work
Reading: Source sheet
Writing: Notes about the success of the Roman army

Learning styles used:
Auditory
Visual
Kinaesthetic

Content: (identify any key questions/key words)	
What does the teacher do?	**What does the pupil do?**
Get class in and settled (08:43)	
Starter: As a starter we are going to see what we already know about the Roman army – read the statements and circle true or false (3 minutes – take register during this time). Ask for hands up for each statement (08:50)	Pupils complete starter activity
Introduce today's learning objective: why was the Roman army so successful? What does successful mean? What do we know that the Roman army did? Conquered lots of places – Caesar [France and Britain]. What types of things would we need to know about the Roman army in order to decide if they were successful? Teacher writes ideas onto board – directs pupils to main areas we will be looking at during the lesson: • What soldier wears • Who is in the army • Organization, training and weapons (08:55)	Pupils listen to learning objectives and contribute to class discussion

Lesson Planning

Activity 1: 'Top Gear: what did Roman soldiers wear?' 3 minutes to complete activity, check answer with A3 Roman soldier on board, ask for pupils to get up and circle the different parts of the uniform (09:03)

Hand out 'Who was in the Roman army?'

Activity 2: 'Who's who?' Explain the task. Students will have 9 minutes to complete it, check answers using pictures on board (2 minutes) (09:14)

Activity 3: Tell pupils to turn to Venn diagram, explain that we are going to look at a number of resources and decide if they tell us about organization, training or weapons. Teacher will read source 1 – pose question 'what does this tell us?', tell pupils to highlight sections with coloured pencils. Read through rest of sources, asking for volunteers and discussing each source after it has been read or looked at (09:22)

Activity 4: Fill in diagram (10 minutes). As this class has a massive range of abilities introduce idea that some of the successes of the Roman army fall under more than one category or all three. More able pupils will be able to identify these

Draw to a close at 09:32. Students state which areas they think are important (09:35)

(Extension task for the more able students, or colouring in and

Pupils match the correct number with the correct statement
Pupils will volunteer to come up to the board and show the rest of the class what different parts of soldier's uniform are

Pupils will cut up the six boxes, them and match the description with the correct picture
Pupils will feed back to the class

Pupils will listen to explanation of Venn diagram
Pupils will listen to teacher reading source 1 and contribute to what it shows us about the army's successes
Pupils will volunteer to read other sources and contribute to what they show us about the army's successes
Pupils will annotate source sheet

Pupils will fill in Venn diagram

Pupils will contribute to class discussion

labelling the soldier on the front cover for those pupils that will get bored of 10 minutes of writing – Carl, Chad, Andy, Karl, Kyle, Stuart)	
(09:35) Plenary – Return to 'True or False' – hopefully all get correct answers!	Pupils will complete True or False activity

Differention by:	Risk Factors:
Task: X Resource: X	**None**
Support: X	

Key Skills:	Literacy X	Numeracy:	I. Technology

Resources: Why was the Roman army so successful? Booklet; Why was the Roman army so Successful? Source sheet; Who's who in the Roman army? Worksheet; Pens; Pencils; Scissors; Glue

Homework: None set today

Lesson Planning

RELIGIOUS EDUCATION

Title: Introduction to Christianity

Date: 7/1
Class: 7O
Ability: Mixed
Period: 5
Length: 60 minutes

Aim and link with previous learning
Introduce 'Christianity in action' unit by thinking about how Christianity affects a Christian's life

Intended learning objectives	Intended learning outcomes
By the end of the lesson students will:	By the end of the lesson:
(LEARN ABOUT)	
Know: That Christianity affects every part of a Christian's life	All students will know that Christianity affects every part of a Christian's life
Understand: How holding individual beliefs affects actions and feelings in specific ways	Most students will think about how their interests and hobbies affect their identities
(LEARN FROM) Think about/reflect upon: How their interests and hobbies affect their identities	Some students will understand how holding individual beliefs affects actions and feelings in specific ways

Activities/Strategies/Differentiation

Whole class	+	**Learning styles**		**Resources**
Group		Visual		See below
Pairs		Auditory	+	
Individual	+	Kinaesthetic		

Assessment opportunities:
During the lesson
Discussion   After the lesson
Worksheet

Homework: None

Lesson delivery plan

Timing	Sequence of activities	Pupil code	Resources/ comments
5	Settle class	B	
6	Introduce myself – give out books and set class rules	L	
	Today we're starting a new module on Christianity in action – refer to aim. However, we're going to start with something different …	L	
4	Write title and date in exercise book. get them to write three favourite hobbies or interests, and circle one which is most important. (register)	B	Exercise books
5	Now, I have a hobby – music. I like hip hop music, and I'm in a band, and that is an important hobby for me. Now, you can usually tell how important a hobby is from how much time it takes up, so I thought of a normal day and how much time music took up in my day.	L	Whiteboard
8	I'd like you to do the same	B	Worksheets
3	Feedback	Q/a	
10	What about a Christian then? Let's do this together. Fill in table	Q/a	
2	OBJECTIVES So a Christian doesn't just do Christian things, like it was a hobby. A Christian's beliefs affect every part of their lives. As we do this unit of work, we don't just want to know	3	

	some things about Christianity but understand what makes Christians tick. We need to ask ourselves not just 'what does a Christian do?' but how would a Christian's beliefs make him or her feel? Or how would it cause a Christian to treat other people. But, we can't ask those questions without knowing what a Christian believes, so turn to Sue Penney, p. 6.		
3	Rd p. 6 – 'what do Christians believe > ... end of the world'	R	Sue Penny book
10	Answer questions on back of sheet	B	
4	Pack away Feedback – how might it affect your life if you thought God was your friend? If you thought God was coming to judge the world?	Q/a	

Pupil code (activities): L = Listening to teacher, Q/a = Questions and answer teacher, D = Pupil discussion together, W = Watching, P = Practical work, B = Book work, Dr = Drama based work, C = Other creative work, e.g. Poetry, drawing, painting, modelling

Christianity in Action

How a Christian's belief affects his/her life

Context of lesson

This was my first lesson of this unit and my first lesson with my three Year 7 classes – 7O, 7G and 7W. I was not overly happy with the unit's suggested beginning, as there seemed very little to link it to the children's experience (especially those who were not brought up in the Christian tradition) and also as the course took a fairly piecemeal approach to Christianity and did not touch on the core Christian beliefs. My aim then was to provide a context for the rest of the course (the importance of the Bible to Christians and various Bible teachings). I wanted to do two things in this endeavour: present Christianity as a living faith, so that future subject matter could be brought alive in the pupils' minds, and also to at least introduce the pupils to central Christian beliefs.

Overall Evaluation

This lesson set out to achieve quite a lot and on the whole was a great success with each of the three groups I taught. The lack of a definite starter to focus the pupils as they arrived was unfortunate, but with each class, the introduction of a new teacher seemed to provide the initial impetus to engage from the start.

The main body of the lesson, focusing on the pupils' hobbies and interests and how they relate to a Christian's faith, successfully captured most pupils' imagination but, with my first class, 7O, the link with Christianity proved a little conceptual for some pupils. Also, I found that I'd take it for granted that pupils would have obvious hobbies and interests, but this proved not to be true in several cases. These two flaws in the lesson were addressed with the next class, 7G, as I explained the task much more clearly and also explained what interests might qualify as hobbies. These clearer instructions meant that at least 90% of the pupils understood the task and understood the link with Christianity as well.

The rest of the lesson was spent doing a comprehension exercise on a page from a textbook about the basic Christian beliefs. This exercise was a suitable one and most pupils completed it well. However, in retrospect, I wonder whether my idea of tacking foundational Christian beliefs on to the end of the lesson was unwise. I think it would have been good to spend a whole lesson, at least, looking at what Christians believe about Jesus and salvation, as to understand 'Christianity in action' it is essential to fully get to grips with the basic Christian belief system. Having said this, a satisfactory number of pupils managed to link this part of the lesson to the earlier part and gave some insightful answers to questions such as 'how might it affect someone's life if they believed God was their friend?'

Another positive element of the latter section of this lesson was the question sheet that I devised. I feel that the questions were appropriate and helpful. Although I did not produce a differentiated worksheet, the

Lesson Planning

questions themselves allowed pupils of different abilities to engage with the task and I offered an extension question to those who finished early. The pacing of these lessons seemed to work, although a more developed plenary would have been helpful. In two of the three classes I got a chance to reinforce learning by asking questions to the class about how various core Christian beliefs may affect a Christian's life, but this only included those who put their hands up and didn't really gauge the general understanding of the class.

Class management was not a problem in any of these three lessons, and I think that this was, in part, because I introduced my expectations clearly at the beginning of each lesson ('hands up before you speak', 'no talking when someone else is speaking') and enforced them consistently.

PHYSICAL EDUCATION

Date 14/1
Time: 8.55–9.55
Activity: Basketball
Venue: Sports Hall
Class: Year 7 boys
No. of Pupils: 26
Unit lesson no: 3
Length of lesson: 1 hour

Objectives: By the end of the lesson pupils …	**Should know and understand:** what muscles need to be stretched before basketball lesson and how to stretch them effectively
	Should be able to: dribble a basketball accuratel without pressure from defenders
Equipment:	13 basketballs, bibs, cones
Non-participants:	Word search worksheet and help with officiating games
Additional information: (to make notes or comments as required, e.g.: assessment methods, aspect of level description, teaching/learning style, management & organization issues such as use of space, groupings, use of AFL strategies, ICT, SEN, risk, etc.)	Command Style Teaching. Assessment for Learning Strategies: effective questioning during and at end of lesson. Open questions, adequate answering time.

Lesson Planning

Time	Learning Activities and Organization	Teaching Points	Differentiation
8.55		Ensure all jewellery off and chewing gum out	
9.05	Register Lesson Objectives: • Re-cap passes • Test knowledge of how to warm-up safely and effectively, in particular which muscles to stretch and how • Dribbling techniques • Dribbling under pressure and awareness of space	Use of effective questioning (assessment for learning)	Choose different pupils to answer, not just those with hands up
9.10	Warm-up: 6 teams of 4/5 – relays 1. Running × 2, then static stretches 2. Right hand dribble (chest pass to next player in line) 3. Left hand dribble (bounce pass to next player in line) 4. Alternate hand dribble (overhead pass to next player in line) 5. Race dribbling, any of 3 types above	Question: What muscles do we stretch and how? Re-cap teaching points for passes, e.g. step in, fingers spread wide behind ball, follow through in direction of partner, bent elbows to straight elbows Dribble T.P.s: • Strong wrist • Cushion ball with palm • To the side of body and slightly in front. Hip	Highlight that the relays are not a race until number 5, therefore removing pressure and concentrating on technique Extension: quicken pace, work non-dominant hand Support: Reduce dribbling and passing distance Extension:

	Main activity: dribbling Follow my leader in coned area (approx. 20 m²) → walking → jogging → running	height • Spatial awareness • Control of ball	smaller coned area. More emphasis on looking up to improve spatial awareness.
9.25	Traffic lights game in coned area 20 m² In pairs One dribbles inside area while partner is jogging around outside of area. Swap over on whistle. Teacher holds up coloured cone, each one signals change of speed. Green = dribble on the move Amber = dribble on the spot Red = stop standing still, holding the ball	• Alternate hands dribbling • Eyes looking ahead while dribbling • Spatial awareness – where are others around me? • Improvement of hand–eye co-ordination	Support: begin task by calling coloured cones as well as holding them up, progress to just holding cones up Extension: work in smaller area
9.30	Dribble – steal the game in coned 20 m² area In pairs One dribbles inside area while partner is jogging around outside of area. Swap over on whistle. All players in area have a ball	Pupils can be teachers and hold coloured cones up. • Pupils must be aware of rules in basketball to steal and protect the ball, i.e. run through contact and double	Extension: limit which hand they can dribble and steal with. Limit space of coned area that they can play in

121

	to dribble except 2 thieves whose aim is to steal the ball off the players, within rules of the game. If thieves steal ball, they must dribble to outside the area, then the dribbler can retrieve the ball back. Thieves cannot steal same player's ball twice in a row. Every time the thieves steal a player's ball, that player gets one point. Aim is for pairs to get least number of points to win.	dribble rule • Eyes up – awareness of where thieves and other players are • Dribble close to body in order to control ball • Protection of ball through quick feed and placement of body	
9.35	Plenary question and answer session to check pupils' learning. Concentrate on assessment for learning strategies.	Example question: What are the three passes used in basketball? Tell me three points about dribbling techniques? Explain two rules of basketball.	Pick on pupils to answer questions, do not rely on hands up
9.40	Cool-down: static stretching	Question: How long do we hold stretches in the cool-down? Why are they held longer?	Choose a different pupil to lead each stretch, therefore building up their knowledge and confidenee of stretches
9.45	Change and re-distribute valuables		

Extension (in case of additional time) 4/5 v 4/5 Conditioned game across width of sports hall. Passing and dribbling skills only, no goals, therefore no shooting. To score must get ball past	Focus on dribbling and passing skills, making the right decision. Teacher to question and discuss decisions made.	3 games in sports hall. Ability group each game.

Lesson Planning

GEOGRAPHY

(KS3 taught in form, KS4 in option blocks)	**Points from previous lesson:**
Class: 8 No. Co Date: 16/3/ Lesson: Wild Weather – 8 **Topic: Wild Weather – Drought**	Introduction to drought case study – Ethiopia
Lesson Objectives: 1) To reinforce Ethiopia case study with video and photos. 2) To use 'guided visualization' to encourage pupils to think about causes and effects of drought and to summarize topic.	
IEP Names and Stages: **Support Staff:** **Role of Support Staff:** N/A	
Resources and materials (including IEP): Brainstorm worksheets, video, PowerPoint presentation, guided visualization, A4 plain paper, books, H/W sheet	
Time	**Activity**
1.25	Pupils enter (often a few at a time from lunch, so starter on desk for pupils to begin as they arrive). Starter – rotating images of drought and famine on PowerPoint. Pupils to brainstorm how the pictures make them feel. Scan room to ensure all are on task. Get feedback from a few pupils.
1.35	State that they have given their thoughts on the photos but now we're going to look at what

1.40	someone who has actually been out there and seen it first-hand thinks. Show 'Bob Geldof' video. Ask how people felt about that – Do they have any questions on the video?
1.50	Plenary – question and answer. Read passage on human effects of drought. Ask pupils to complete a series of pictures (worksheet) that identify the major causes and effects of drought. Pupils hold up their drawings. Get pupils to give feedback on what they have learnt about drought.
2.05	Give out and explain homework – day in the life of Amna.
Assessment Criteria H/W how well they have understood topic. Involvement in class work/discussions.	

Lesson Planning

MODERN FOREIGN LANGUAGES

Date: 18 November

Class: 8B1   **Ability: High**   **No. of Pupils: 32**

Resources: Simpson family flash cards
Board Pen
Blu Tack
'Famous people' cards

Previous lesson: Finished the first unit of the book.

Aims and Learning Objective: To introduce the second unit: 'La Famille'. To introduce il and elle – thus the forms il/elle s'appelle and il/elle a ... ans'. To learn mom, dad, brother and sister (and note which ones are masculine and feminine – le/la.) To learn: 'As-tu des freres et des soeurs?' To learn how to respond, in the positive (saying 1/2/3, etc., brothers and sisters, and in the negative, saying 'Je n'ai pas de frères ni de soeurs'. For the latter, they will also learn 'je suis fille unique'. Depending on how well they cope, I will explain 'je suis fils unique' as well, although they won't need this personally, it reinforces the masculine/feminine.

Timing	Activities	A.T. levels	P.o.S
	As a starter I will do a quick re-run of Joan's previous revision session, in order to bring the 'je m'appelle' and 'ja'ai ... ans' phrases back into everyone's minds. At this point, if there is anyone who has not yet written this information into their books, I will get them to do it. I will then introduce il and elle using stick people on the board and using the cognates masculine and feminine, as well as pointing to myself and saying 'je' so that they become aware that I am looking for a pronoun, to explain what they mean. Once this has been established I will remind them of 'je m'appelle ...' and 'j'ai ... ans'. I'll then point back to my stick people and say write 'Pierre' '12' next to the boy, and 'Marie' '11' next to the girl. I will say the information and then say 'comment se dit en françias?'	1:1–2 2:2 1:1–2	1a, b 2a,b,c,f,i 3b,c 5a 1a,b 2a,b,c,d, g,i 3b,c 5a

pointing to the brief information. I will
then give them the answer orally,
pointing to the boy, saying 'IL S'appelle
Pierre' 'IL A 12 ans'. I will ask them
to translate then I'll chorus the
phrases a few times before doing the | 2:2
same with the girl. When it's been
chorused sufficiently, and they all know
what it means, I'll write the date, | 1a,b
weather and title on the board, and | 2a,b,c,d,
get them to copy the information | g,i
into their books. I'll have written on the
board so that they can copy it directly.
I will then introduce the family member | 3:2 | 3b,c
by using the Simpsons flash cards. I'll | 4:2–3 | 5a
introduce Lisa, saying 'elle s'appelle
Lisa'. I'll stick her on the board and
then show Bart, saying 'Il s'appelle
Bart, Bart est LE FRERE de Lisa'. I'll
repeat this a few times, pointing to | 1a,b
both characters then I'll ask what it
means. Once they've answered I'll do | 1:2
the same with Maggie, introducing | 2:2–3 | 2a,b,c,e,
'soeure'. | f,g
I will do the same style of introducing | 3b,c
for Marge and Homer – 'mère' and | 1:2 | 5a
'père'. We will do more chorusing and
then we will write the vocab down,
writing masculine words in blue and
feminine in red. I will point to the
colours (and the le/la) and ask
'pourquoi le/la'? After having learnt
'il/elle' earlier, and having the flash
cards on the board to help, they should
explain the difference. We will then
chorus once more and they will write it | 1:2–3 | 1a,b
in their books. I'll then introduce the | 2:2–3 | 2a,b,c,e,
question 'As-tu des frères ou des | f,g
soeurs?' I'll take the Lisa flash card off
the board and pretend to be | 3b,c
Lisa, saying 'je m'appelle Lisa. J'ai un | 5a
frère (pointing at Bart) et (pointing to
Maggie) une soeur.' I'll ask the class
what I have just said, doing it again if
necessary. We will then chorus the
phrases. I'll then stick the card back | 1:2

Lesson Planning

on the board and I'll point to myself, saying 'moi, moi', whilst shaking my head and saying 'non, je n'ai pas de frères ni de soeurs, je suis une fille unique'. I will repeat this and then ask what it means. We will chorus it and then write iton the board. I will write 'fille unique' in red and then look at the class pointing to me, saying 'une fille unique'. I'll then point back to my stick man, and say 'IL est UN FILS unique'.	2:2	1a,b,c 2a,b,c,e, f,i 3b,c
I'll repeat both phrases, pointing to me and the stick man when necessary, and then ask 'Qu'est-ce que c'est fille unique?' Once answered I'll ask, 'Qu'est-ce que c'est fils unique?' pointing to the boy. Once they've answered I'll write the masculine form on the board. I'll draw one stick boy with the singular affirmative phrase, then draw two with the plural, I'll do the same with one/two girls and then I'll write the negative answers. Whilst I'm doing this I'll have set the class the task to work in pairs, asking each other the question. I will then get the girls to copy the information from the board into their books (miming the action whilst saying the cognate 'copier'). As a plenary I will introduce the 'famous people' cards. They have a card with a famous person's name on it. The girls have to adopt the role of that person and, depending on how many stick people there are on the card, they have to say how many brothers/sisters they have (or answer in the negative if necessary). I'll give them a few minutes to complete this exercise, then I will bring the class together to explain their homework.	3:2–3 4:2–3	5a
I will emphasize the verb 'apprendre' whilst writing 'to learn' on the board. I will tell them to learn the vocab, from the text book and to do exercise 5a & b	1:3	1a,b 2a,b,c

	from p.17 of the activity book. I will show them the exercise, and if necessary write it in English. I'll get someone who has understood to explain to the rest of the class. I will then collect in the exercise books to mark last lesson's homework. Once collected in, I will dismiss them one row at a time.	2:3–4	e,f,h
			3b,c,e
			5a,d
		1:3–4	
			3e
		3:2–3	
		4:2–3	
			5a

Lesson Planning

ENGLISH

Date:

Lesson No:

Scheme of work: Novel 'Friedrick' by Hans Peter Richter.

Aim of lesson (plus homework): ICT use to improve the quality and detail of pupils' autobiographies.

Learning outcomes – conceptual:
For pupils to be able to plan and draft their writing on screen. Use ICT to explore and develop ideas.

Concrete: Using ICT to structure pupils' work. ICT to develop pupils' awareness of how to plan and the importance of doing so. ICT to improve the quality of pupils' work.

NC areas being addressed: En3 2a En3 2b	Framework coverage: Writing 1 Writing 3	
Starter:	Whole class discussion of the features of writing an autobiography (previously visited). One pupil to scribe the features discussed on the Interactive board so the pupils have access to them throughout the lesson.	Clock/time 10
Whole Class Activity:	Introduce the task – using ICT to improve the quality and detail of work by planning before writing. Explain how the lesson will work – I will model tasks throughout, so it is essential for pupils to be listening and watching as I show them how. INSTRUCTIONS: • Open a Microsoft Word document (model this on the Interactive board for all the pupils to see *how* to do this) • Select 'view' on the menu and then 'outline' in the drop down menu.	5
Stage 1 – paragraph level	Advise pupils that they will be structuring their ideas on a paragraph level. They have 1 minute to put a single point for each paragraph. Model the task – my first	

130

	childhood memory is riding my bike. Once they have done this, the pupils need to press ENTER and then simply type what happened in their next paragraph (reminder that this did not need to be a new memory). For example: falling off my bike. Pupils need to keep doing this until they have the main ideas for their four memories. Set the Interactive stopwatch and give pupils only 1 minute to do this.	5
Stage 2 – sentence level	Model task – pupils need to put their cursor at the end of the first line they typed and press ENTER. On the toolbar, to the right of 'Level 1' will be an arrow pointing right. The pupils need to click this to 'demote' the point to 'level 2'. Advise the pupils to type in their first piece of detail for this paragraph. Model the task – for paragraph 1 – riding my bike, write under it 'learning to ride my bike in the park with my mum and dad'. For the next paragraph, add the detail 'my dad took off the training wheels and promised he would not let go of me. He did and I fell.' For each new piece of detail for the paragraph, the pupils need to have pressed ENTER. Put 4 minutes on the stopwatch to do this.	10
Stage 3 – word level	Pupils need to place their cursor at the end of the **sentence** level line this time and press ENTER. Then demote the 'level 2' to level 3 by clicking the right arrow (model this for pupils). For each of the sentence level ideas, pupils need to think of key words or descriptive phrases which would be good to use. Put 5 minutes on the stopwatch for this.	10
Individual task	Advise pupils they need to go back to the 'view' menu and select 'normal' (model this on Interactive board). Pupils will see that their paragraph ideas are in large bold writing. Underneath are the sentence ideas in bold and finally,	

Lesson Planning

	underneath them the individual words in a smaller print. Give pupils time to draft their work and put their ideas into proper sentences and paragraphs. Pupils to save their work as shown in the instructions on the whiteboard.	15
End of lesson	Plenary: With the person sitting next to them, pupils to discuss the ways in which ICT in English has helped them, if at all (and be honest!). Pupils to write these points on the post-it note handed out.	10

Notes – including information about materials, resources, classroom arrangements, etc.

Resources:
- Computers
- Task and Objectives on Interactive whiteboard

Classroom arrangements:
- One pupil per computer, pupils to be seated beside the person they worked with
  in usual lessons

Assessment intentions and opportunities, in line with assessment objectives and NC

Discussion during the Starter – already looked at examples of auto-biographies – pupils to pool together their ideas of how one should be written, debating on its features. I will simply facilitate the discussion, scribing what the pupils say, inputting only when asked. Plenary – pair work for pupils to share their ideas of what they really think. This will allow pupils to consider other points of view and the written notes on the post-it will allow me to anonymously assess the success or lack of, of using ICT for planning/drafting.

Evaluation of lesson – focus on what the pupils learned and/or achieved in relation to lesson plan

In this lesson, I wanted to use ICT to improve the quality and detail of the pupils' work. In previous lessons I had noticed that the pupils were very resistant to planning. They simply completed a spider diagram with very little detail, which they then failed to use when writing. When completing written activities, the pupils simply wrote off the top of their head which resulted in them producing work with very little detail, the quality of which was also very poor. After trying and failing to help the pupils learn the importance of planning to improve the quality of their work, I decided to use ICT to help the pupils construct a well-written piece of text.

There were many benefits to this lesson and a lot of negative aspects too. This task was very tiring. At times as I modelled the task on the Interactive board, there was at least one pupil who had not been paying attention. This resulted in the rest of the class being held up as I reinforced the instructions. After a while this became very tiresome and I became very frustrated with certain pupils, who found the prospect of exploring various buttons on the computer more interesting than following instructions. As well as this, I learnt that a task such as this one can only be carried out with a class who are well behaved. I think it is impossible to do such a task without considering that certain hiccups will occur as it is impossible for pupils not to fiddle with computers when they should be listening.

I also misjudged the timing in the lesson. I was only able to book the computer suite for one lesson as this was the only time the lesson coincided with a free room. Due to this, many pupils did not manage to complete their autobiographies which I felt rendered the process of planning ineffective as most pupils did not get to use their plans.

Having argued this through, there were some beneficial aspects to this lesson. First of all, using the stopwatch on the Interactive board was a good idea as during the 'structuring' aspect of the lesson, the pupils were motivated by the ticking of the clock. As well as this, I believe that if I had not modelled the entire lesson on the Interactive board for all the pupils to see, the entire lesson would have been a lot more difficult that it actually was.

The pupils seemed to enjoy the task a lot and I have high expectations of the quality of the work the pupils will produce. When circulating, I glanced through some of the work they had done and it appeared to be very good.

Having looked at the notes the pupils wrote on the post-its during the plenary, I have found that all the pupils felt that ICT had been extremely useful. They not only enjoyed using it but many commented that it made them see how useful planning could be for their writing.

I did not hold a whole class discussion for the plenary although I had considered it. This is because there are many pupils in this class who are often reluctant to say how they really feel in front of the rest of the class. Other pupils I feel tend to predict what they believe I want to hear, which results in me not actually knowing anything about the pupils' learning needs. However, asking pupils their opinions of using ICT in pairs and to note these on post-its for privacy, provided the opportunity for pupils to confer, share ideas and anonymously write how they feel. My aim is to use the pupils' views of how ICT in English has helped them or has not helped then and to address these issues in the next lesson.

Overall, I feel that using ICT has been very effective as it has helped to improve the detail and quality of the pupils' work.

Appendix 1: Competencies in planning and preparation

1. You should be able to plan and prepare lessons using your knowledge and understanding of:
   - the knowledge, concepts and skills of the subjects you are teaching;
   - the requirements of the National Curriculum, GCSE syllabus and/or AS/A2 specifications in the subjects you are teaching;
   - the overall structure of the schemes you are currently teaching.

2. You should be able to plan and prepare lessons that are appropriate to the needs of the individuals and groups you teach, and provide progression and continuity of learning by:
   - setting achievable learning objectives;
   - building on students' previous learning;
   - differentiating tasks (on the basis of level of difficulty, pace of work, classroom support and learning styles).

3. You should be able to plan and prepare lessons that take account of the development of the students as 'whole' persons by:
   - contributing to the development of students' literacy, numeracy and oracy skills;
   - taking into account, where relevant, the cross-curricular themes as identified in the National Curriculum;

- developing social skills alongside academic skills in the process of learning;
- taking account of the contribution different subject areas make to the whole curriculum.

4. You should be able to enhance the students' knowledge, understanding and skills through:
   - the use of resources that are appropriate to the objectives being taught;
   - the appropriate use of resources in relation to the learning activities within a phase of a lesson.

5. You should be able to consult and plan with support staff by:
   - knowing where to go for help and advice about students who have special needs;
   - having a clear understanding of the roles of learning support staff within your school.

Source: Based on a competency profile contained in Tolley, H., Biddulph, M. and Fisher, T. (1996).

Appendix 2: The influence of the National Strategies on lesson planning

The Literacy, Numeracy and Key Stage 3 National Strategies, sequentially introduced in the late 1990s, have had an impact on raising standards and strengthening teaching and learning across the National Curriculum in England and Wales. One of the areas of particular influence has been on the structuring of learning, with a significant emphasis on planning lessons. Here the key focus has been upon the use of starters and plenaries, the introduction of more challenge into the learning experience and the greater engagement of students in the learning tasks.

The support materials which accompany the Foundation Subject Strategy state, quite rightly, that:

> Good planning underpins good practice. It helps to ensure that teaching is focused on what students need to learn to make good progress.
>
> (DfES/QCA, 2002, p. 66)

These materials also clarify the purpose of lesson planning as helping teachers to:

- Structure their lessons.
- Build on previous lessons and learning.
- Share the objectives of the lesson with students.
- Assess student achievements.
- Develop effective assessment for learning.
- Make lessons more inclusive and address a range of needs.

Appendix 2

- Make better use of classroom support.
- Make explicit the key strategies they wish to use.
- Address the key questions they need to ask.
- Highlight key vocabulary.
- Focus on targets for raising standards, including literacy, numeracy and ICT.
- Set homework.

(DfES/QCA, 2002, p. 66)

References

Some of the material in this book draws upon sections of an earlier book I wrote for Continuum titled *Reflective Teaching of Geography 11–18*.

Battersby, J. (1995) *Teaching Geography at Key Stage 3*. Cambridge: Chris Kington Publishing.

Bennetts, T. (1996) 'Planning your courses', in Bailey, P. and Fox, P. (eds) *Geography Teachers' Handbook*. Sheffield: Geographical Association, 49–63.

Blum, P. (1998) *Surviving and Succeeding in Difficult Classrooms*. London: Routledge.

Capel, S., Leask, M. and Turner, T. (1999) *Learning to Teach in the Secondary School*. London: Routledge.

Cohen, L., Manion, L. and Morrison, K. (1996) *A Guide to Teaching Practice*. London: Routledge.

DfES (2002) *Extending Opportunities: Raising Standards*. London: HMSO.

DfES (2002a) *Training materials for the Foundation Subjects*. London: DfES.

DfES (2004) *Pedagogy and Practice: Teaching and Learning in Secondary Schools. Unit 1: Structuring Learning. Key Stage 3 National Strategy*. London: HMSO.

DfES/QCA (2002) *Training materials for the Foundation Subjects: Module 3. Lesson Planning*. London: DfES.

Elliott, P. (2004) 'Planning for learning', in Brooks, V., Abbott, A. and Bills, L. (eds) *Preparing to Teach in Secondary Schools: A Student Teacher's Guide to Professional Issues in Secondary Education*. Maidenhead: Open University Press.

Ferretti, J. (2005) 'Challenging gifted geographers', *Teaching Geography* **30** (2), 82–5.

References

Gardner, H. (1983) *Frames of Mind: The Theory of Multiple Intelligences*. New York: Basic Books.

Grey, D. (2001) *The internet in school*. London: Continuum.

Hyman, P. (2005) *1 out of 10: from Downing Street vision to classroom reality*. London: Vintage.

Kyriacou, C. (1986) *Effective Teaching in Schools*. Oxford: Blackwell.

Kyriacou, C. (1995) *Essential Teaching Skills*. Cheltenham: Stanley Thorne.

Moore, A. (2000) *Teaching and Learning: Pedagogy, Curriculum and Culture*. London: RoutledgeFalmer.

O'Brien, J. and Guiney, D. (2001) *Differentiation in Teaching and Learning: Principles and Practice*. London: Continuum.

Prestage, S., Perks, P. and Hewitt, D. (2005) Lesson Planning and Evaluation. Unpublished paper. Birmingham: University of Birmingham.

Shulman, L. (1999) 'Knowledge and teaching: foundations of the new reform', in Leach, J. and Moon, B. (eds) *Learners and Pedagogy*. London: Paul Chapman/Open University, 61–77.

Tolley, H., Biddulph, M. and Fisher, T. (1996) *Workbook 2: Beginning Initial Teacher Training*. Cambridge: Chris Kington Publishing.

Waters, A. (1995) 'Differentiation and classroom practice', *Teaching Geography* **20** (2), 81–4.